EYES
ON THE
PRIZE

EYES
ON THE
PRIZE

**A KICK-ASS GUIDE
TO SETTING & ACHIEVING
G.R.E.A.T. GOALS**

CARRIE WILLIAMS

ISBN-13: 9780692898222
ISBN-10: 0692898220
Library of Congress Control Number: 2017943880
RainShadow Coaching, Lake Balboa, CA

More advance reviews:

"I struggle with being so busy, I lose my focus on the big things. Carrie drills down on exactly what it is that holds each of us back from operating at a higher level and going after the greatness that we are all capable of."

ANNA VOCINO, COMEDIAN AND COOKBOOK AUTHOR

"Carrie's book shines the light in dark places and illuminates what's hidden. A few short chapters and you will 'see' what's been holding you back. More importantly she gives you the tools to transform the darkness into light! Spectacular, super easy and revealing. All the confusion disappeared at the first read."

SHIVANI GRAIL, ENTREPRENEUR

"A must read! G.R.E.A.T. goal setting works. No more excuses…it's time to get started reaching your goals! Carrie Williams shows us all how we can reframe excuses into challenges we can overcome."

MARY B. LUCAS, STAFFING INDUSTRY EXECUTIVE, SPEAKER, COACH, AND AUTHOR OF *LUNCHMEAT & LIFE LESSONS*

"This book by Carrie Williams is THE manual for training your mind, heart, and body to be an achiever. It provides not just theory, but daily practices to literally re-wire your mind."

ELIZABETH FRISCH, FOUNDER OF THE THRIVAL COMPANY AND AMAZON BEST-SELLING AUTHOR OF *MISSION TO MILLION$: TAKING BIG IDEAS AND MAKING THEM REALITY*

Disclaimer

The names in this book have been changed, and stories and situations have been modified, combined, or created to protect the confidentiality of individuals.

Results achieved by individuals in this book are not necessarily typical. Individual results with coaching are dependent on the individual.

Coaching is not therapy, nor should it be used as such. If you are feeling depressed or suicidal, please seek the help of a licensed therapist.

Acknowledgments

Writing this book has been my own G.R.E.A.T. Goal for the past few years, and I would like to thank a few people for helping me achieve it:

- My husband, Matt, who challenges me to be better and dream bigger and who supports me on all my journeys no matter how long they may take. I am proud to be part of Team Williams
- My clients, who trust me to walk alongside them on the goal-setting journey
- My editors, Anne Erickson, Heather Marsh, and Jaqueline Kyle, for helping me say what I really mean and deleting my exclamation points
- My parents and sisters, for allowing me to be my crazy, goal-loving self and for listening to my big plans
- My friends and colleagues, specifically Leigh Mires and Julia Rothstein, for inspiring me intellectually and reminding me that powerful women can change the world
- My other sister, Katie Fitzmaurice, for her talented illustrations

My heart is full of gratitude for all those who helped me along the way.

Table of Contents

One

Your Journey Begins

W hat do you want in life?
What are you doing every day to make your dreams your reality?

If you can't answer these two questions with confidence and pride...

If you can't answer without hesitation or doubt...

This is the book for you.

This book is also for you if

- you don't know what you want, you just know what you have isn't enough;
- you have an idea of where you want to be but aren't sure how to get there; or
- you absolutely know what you want and how to get there, but you aren't doing what you need to do to make it happen.

By the time you are finished reading this book, you will know the answers to these questions and so much more.

The fact that you are reading this book means you are ready to make a change. It means you recognize that there is more for you in life, and you are *not* willing to sit back and wait for someone to give it to you. You are ready to make it happen! I could tell you that you will use the skills you learn from reading this book for the rest of your life, but I'm not going to. I'll let you discover that for yourself. So let's get started.

G.R.E.A.T. Goals is a system. With this system, I will take you through the process that has been used successfully by hundreds of my coaching clients to identify their dreams, set impactful goals, create a step-by-step action plan, and follow that plan to success. G.R.E.A.T Goals will empower you to embrace your dreams and commit to their fulfillment. Every day my clients achieve more for themselves, their families, and their communities by working the steps outlined in this program.

As a leadership and executive coach in Los Angeles, California, I have worked with thousands of clients both in the entertainment industry and in the "real" world. Helping clients clarify their personal and business goals and finding tangible, measurable ways to evaluate their progress and success led me to the creation of the G.R.E.A.T Goals program. It has been fifteen years in the making, but I am proud to share this book and these strategies with you. There is nothing more fulfilling to me than helping clients discover, then achieve, their goals.

This book is based on two simple premises:

1. You deserve to feel fulfilled and live your passion.
2. You have the potential to make your dreams your reality.

Sit with these ideas for a minute. How do these statements feel in your gut? Most of my clients have a problem with, or a reaction to, at least one. I'll bet you do, too. Maybe you don't feel deserving. Maybe you don't know where or how to start. Perhaps you are unsure of your capabilities. Perhaps you doubt you can live the life you dream about. You might want to believe, but past experiences or the voices in your head won't let you yet. That's okay.

You don't need to believe those two statements are true for this process to work. You just have to be open to the possibility that they're true. At this point I am not asking you to have faith; I am just asking you to have hope—and to keep reading. Keep reading with an open mind.

You deserve to feel fulfilled and live your passion. You can make your dreams your reality. I know you will prove these two simple premises are true.

Knowing what you want, setting a goal, and reaching it seems like a simple process: See it. Want it. Achieve it. But if it's so simple, why aren't we all living life to our fullest potential? Why aren't we all happy, fulfilled, thin, and wealthy?

There are only two reasons you haven't reached your goals (yes, only two):

1. You lack the knowledge or skills to set and achieve your goals.
2. You choose not to set and achieve your goals.

That's it. Either you don't know how to, or you choose not to. Which is true for you?

In this book, I will be asking you to participate, answer questions, and analyze your actions and choices. If you want this process to work, you need to be completely honest. I will ask you to look in a metaphorical mirror and acknowledge what you see. It is important that you share the true reflection—not what you hope to see or what you fear you might see but what is actually in front of you. This may seem difficult or uncomfortable at first. For some of you, the experience might be so uncomfortable that you put down this book and never pick it up again. But I encourage you to continue despite the discomfort and reach for the change that is just around the corner.

Embracing Change

Change can be uncomfortable. It's scary to try something new and push beyond your boundaries. It's stressful to acknowledge that your habits, whether they are good or bad, may no longer be working for you and that to get where you want to be, to grow as a person, you may need to discard certain coping mechanisms that have proven useful until now. Simply put, we fear the unknown, and what we fear, we avoid.

A coach I once worked with told me that she learned to relish that little knot of anxiety she felt in her core when she felt fear. Growth requires change, and change can cause fear, so that knot of tension told her she was on the right track. Whenever that knot went away, she knew she was no longer growing and was instead becoming complacent. I'm not asking you to live the rest of your life with a knot in your stomach. I'm merely suggesting that, in some instances, being uncomfortable can be a good thing. Being uncomfortable means you are growing, and that should be embraced, not avoided.

Charting Change

In order to get to where you want to be, we need to accurately pinpoint where you are starting from. We are cartographers drawing a map that will lead you to success, but a map is only useful if you can see both the destination and the starting point. If you only have the destination and not the starting point, you can't determine the first steps you need to take. You don't know how to pace yourself. You can't identify the obstacles that may be in your path and figure out ways to get around them. Conversely, if you only know your starting point, you will have no idea which path or direction will take you to your ultimate destination. You'll simply wander randomly, wasting time and effort, hoping the next turn will lead to something worthwhile.

To get the most benefit from this book, do the exercises freely and to the best of your ability.

You will need to be relentlessly honest with yourself. It is human nature to put a positive spin on things to make them seem better or to put things in a negative light to minimize the stakes. Neither tendency will help you here. To fully embark on the journey toward reaching your goal, an unfiltered personal viewpoint is best.

Instant Results (When you decide to make something happen)

"How long will this process take?" you ask. Many books claim that they can make you

"Lose Ten Pounds in Ten Days,"
"Love Yourself in Twenty-One Days,"
"Make a Million in 365 Days."

I'm sure you've seen similar books. You may even own a few. These books are trying to leverage the modern-day desire for speed. We want results, and we want them yesterday. We no longer use snail mail or even fax—we e-mail. We no longer wait until we get home to listen to our voice mail—we call or text back immediately on a cell phone that we carry with us twenty-four-seven. We no longer grow our own food and spend hours cooking a family dinner. Instead, we hop in the car and get fast food from the drive-through. We like immediate gratification. We crave it, just like we crave that fast food.

These books also tap into the myth that you might have heard about—that you can create a new habit by doing something for twenty-one days in a row. How many of you have tried that only to find that on the twenty-second day you reverted back to your old habit with a sigh of relief and a cringe of guilt? You're not alone. The theory behind this hypothesis is that somewhere within the twenty-one days you will complete the psychological process of transition (a process we will talk more about later in this book), and you will overcome your immunity to change. Transition is the process that allows you to mentally and emotionally embrace and accept change and make it permanent. Change *without* transition is just temporary change. Change *with* transition is a new and permanent habit. Unfortunately, just forcing yourself to do something every day for three weeks is not enough to create true transition and make that change a new reality, especially if you are fighting it every step of the way.

As much as you might crave it, I'm not going to give you a timeline for completing this book and learning these tools. Years of working with clients have taught me that you are the only one who can decide how long this process will take. You can make it as difficult or as simple as you choose. You can zip through it and start using these tools in your life tomorrow, or you can struggle and fight the process and take months before you actually try them.

I'm not giving you a timeline because the schedule is up to you. I have seen clients agonize over a simple task and take years to complete it. I have seen other people reach goals in less than a week that they thought would take months or years. I can't tell you how many times I've heard, "I have been this way all my life, and it will take a lifetime to change," or "It took me a long time to learn this habit; it will take me a long time to unlearn it." If you believe those statements, you will make them true. If you believe change is hard, you will make it hard. If you believe it will take a long time, it will. Part of my job as a coach is to help my clients shift their perspective on change.

Shining Stars

In my coaching practice, I have worked with a vast range of clients and personalities. Every client's process and relationship is unique. Some struggle and fight every step of the process. Some make progress in spurts with periods of rest along the way. Some make strong and steady progress. However, a few make change happen quickly and reach or surpass their goal before even they thought possible. I like to refer to this final group of clients as my Star Clients. I made it a point to study my Star Clients to see if I could find how they created change in their lives so quickly, so I could share that information with my clients who were struggling. I discovered that there were two traits that all of my Stars have in common:

1. They are committed. They give the best they have at any moment. They may not understand the purpose or reason for the task they're given, but they accept that it must be done and complete it wholeheartedly.
2. They recognize when they are getting in their own way, and they move.

I once taught a two-week workshop to a group of aspiring writers designed to help them get unstuck, set a ninety-day goal, and create a plan to reach that goal. At the end of the first week, I looked around the room at every participant and said, "I wonder which of you will come to class next week and will already have accomplished your ninety-day goal? There is always at least one." The class looked at me incredulously. Was I joking? Many of them thought it was impossible to reach their goal by ninety days, but to reach it in seven? I must be crazy. They laughed at me and shook their heads in disbelief.

At the beginning of the second week, we started class by going around the room and sharing our progress. Some people were behind target, some were on target, a few were ahead of target. Each shared their struggles and their successes. Then, the final person stood to share her progress, and she said, "I need to come up with a new goal."

Another classmate asked, "Did you decide you didn't love the goal you set enough to reach it?"

"No, I reached my goal yesterday." Her goal was to edit and rewrite a scientific article and submit it for publishing. "You said at least one person always reaches her goal in a week. At first, I thought that would never happen but then I thought, why not me? So I just did it."

She was able to take a goal she had struggled with for over a year and that she was uncertain she could accomplish in ninety days, and she reached it in six days! She decided to be a "Star," got out of her own way, and committed.

That, my friends, is why I refuse to give you a timeline. Your success all depends on you.

So are you ready to move forward? Are you ready to create your action plan? Are you ready to achieve your G.R.E.A.T. Goals and succeed in ways you never dreamed of before? Read on if you are ready to accept the challenge.

Two

Smart to G.R.E.A.T.

This chapter will explore the differences between being smart and being G.R.E.A.T. For decades, S.M.A.R.T. Goals (Specific, Measurable, Achievable, Reachable, Timely) have been the goal-setting standard in education and business. I say, "Why settle for S.M.A.R.T. when you can be G.R.E.A.T?"

Read on to learn how your mindset can affect your results and how the right mindset can lead to incredible success.

Learning to be Smart

From the time we are infants, we learn from our successes and mistakes, and we change our actions accordingly to get the results we desire. As a baby, if we smiled, someone usually smiled back. If we cried, someone usually changed, fed, or held us. We learned quickly that sometimes there were negative results from our actions. If we drew on the walls, we most likely got a time-out. If we touched the hot pot on the stove, we got burned. If we said a bad word, we got sent to our room, or worse, got a mouthful of soap. We quickly learned that some actions led to reward and others led to pain or punishment.

Growing up, we learned more about choices and consequences. If you did something wrong, some of the worst insults you might have heard as a kid were "dummy," "moron," "stupid," or "idiot." There was nothing more bone-achingly humiliating than to have someone insult your level of intelligence, because surely if they said it, there must be some truth to it. Right? A harsh word taken to heart, even if it's not true, can be enough to redefine your self-image.

As an adult, the negative comments are usually more subtle, but we often react the same way—with self-doubt and second guessing. As a result of these life lessons, we have learned to shift our choices and decisions not only to get what we want but also to avoid what we don't want. We don't want to be criticized. We don't want to be judged. We don't want to disappoint ourselves or others. We learn to be smarter. However, if we're only seeking to avoid other people's disapproval, and we've gotten into the habit of internalizing what other people have said to us over the years, we may have developed some habits that need to be changed. If you believe that you have to be smart all the time, it's possible you are limiting yourself because you can't set your sights higher. You may be missing an opportunity to be more than just smart.

I recently worked with a client who was attending a prestigious college. We were discussing the joys and trials of learning and the challenge of learning something new, and she shared this insight: "I have to take classes I know I can get a good grade in so I can keep my scholarship. Also, my parents who are paying for my education will freak out if I get a bad grade. I can't risk taking a class that I am not sure I can ace, even if it sounds interesting." For her, education was not about growth, challenge, and learning but about proving her level of intelligence and avoiding negative outcomes. She was willing to limit her education and sacrifice her growth to prove how smart she was.

I say…why settle for smart when you can be great?

Smart versus G.R.E.A.T.

Being *smart* means you won't take certain actions because the odds are against you or the risk is too high. Being *great* means you are willing to take a potentially risky action because you know the payoff is worth it.

Being *smart* means you won't make a decision that will most likely end in failure. Being *great* means you recognize that even failure can be a success if you learn and grow from it.

Being *smart* means you will do anything not to be perceived as stupid. Being *great* means you don't care who calls you stupid because you know the truth.

Being *smart* means you are better than the person next to you. Being *great* means you are the best you can be.

Look at the columns below. Are you smart, or are you great? Which do you want to be?

SMART	G.R.E.A.T.
Knows own strengths	Leverages own strengths
Avoids obstacles	Overcomes obstacles
Impresses others	Inspires self and others
Takes advantage of opportunities	Creates opportunities
Able to be better than others	Able to be best self
Knows own limits	Has no limits
Fixed mindset	Growth mindset
Meets expectations	Exceeds expectations

So here is my question: Are you ready to be great? This is a sincere question. Are *you* ready to be *great*? Are you ready to do what it takes to make the necessary changes and to stay focused, even when the process gets hard or uncomfortable? Do you believe that you are worth the time, energy, and growing pains? Are you willing to put in the effort to change your status quo? You have the ability. Remember the two premises of this book? You deserve to feel fulfilled and live your passion. You have the potential to make your dreams your reality. Those are the two elements of greatness.

This means *you* have the ability to be *great*. The question is this: Are you ready to *be* great?

Throughout this book, I will be asking you to participate by doing activities or answering questions. These questions are designed to help you get to your destination and to spur some discoveries along the way. I recommend you designate a notebook specifically for the G.R.E.A.T. Goal Activities and make use of the free companion worksheets and exercises available from my website RainShadowCoaching.com.

There are only two rules with these exercises:

1. You must answer. Your full participation is the key!
2. The answer can't be "I don't know." Give your best guess or what seems to be closest to the truth. "I don't know" is a non-answer and won't help you move forward.

G.R.E.A.T. Goal Activity 2-1
Answer the following questions:

1. What do you hope to gain from this goal-setting process?
2. What will need to change in your life in order to make setting new goals a priority?

3. What will you need to lose or sacrifice in order to make your goals a priority?
4. Is making this sacrifice worth it to you? If not, what would it take to make this sacrifice worthwhile? Why are you willing to make this sacrifice now?

The Mindset of Change

Before we get down to the goal setting, I want to take a moment to share some thoughts about change and the mindset necessary to reach your G.R.E.A.T. Goal.

A person will only change for one of two reasons:

1. They want to
2. They are forced to

The people who fall into the first category can clearly identify what they want and where they want to go. They can see what the end reward will be, the payoff for all their efforts, and it is worth it to them. They are excited and self-motivated.

The people you find in the second category are those who feel like they "have to" change or they "should" change, but they are only creating the actual change so they can avoid a negative outcome. In this case, they are forced to adopt a change in order to avoid a consequence or loss.

Here are a few examples I have come across in my years of coaching; let's see if you can identify which category they belong to. (The names I am using are not those of my actual clients, and their stories, or parts thereof, are being used with their consent. In some cases, traits or situations have been combined or created to make a more concise example.)

Example 1
April was sent to me by her parents. She was a senior in college and was not doing so well with her studies or her plans for the future. She was currently failing a class, and she had taken extensions on two other classes, which were about to run out. If she didn't make some immediate changes, it was likely she would have to take an additional semester of classes as well as summer courses. In addition, April didn't have a clear idea of her career path beyond college. In fact, while she was quick to point out what she didn't want in a job, she had no idea what she did want—except for her parents to relax and get off her back.

Example 2
Mark lost his job due to a company closing over a year before our first session. Since the closing, he had been actively job searching every day and had been on over thirty interviews. Despite being highly qualified for the positions, he was never offered one. Mark wanted to figure out if there was something he could shift or change to make the next interview a success.

Example 3
Amanda was having trouble transitioning to a new job and hoped coaching could help with the process. She worked in a creative field with an incredibly tight team of coworkers, and she didn't feel like she fit in. The other team members had similar values, attitudes, likes and dislikes, while Amanda seemed to differ on everything. In addition, Amanda technically had the bottommost status in the group, being the last hire and the lowest in the hierarchy of power. Her differences caused her to detach from the group, only furthering her feelings of alienation and her personal unhappiness with the position. Amanda was concerned that if something didn't change soon, she would be fired, but she wasn't so sure that would be a bad thing.

Example 4
Emily was a new solo entrepreneur. For over a decade, she had longed to be self-employed, and she had recently become an independent sales rep for a franchise that she loved and believed in. She really wanted to make her solo career a success and had set impressive financial and networking goals for herself in her first year. Emily wanted to make sure she was leveraging her strengths and had a solid plan for her first one hundred days, so she could hit the ground running.

Which people in the above examples are clear about what they are working toward? Can you tell who believes that the end result is worth the effort? These people are changing because *they want to*. By contrast, which of the above are examples of a "have to" or "should" attitude? Who is considering change not for what it brings but for what it avoids? These people are changing because *they are forced to*.

April and Amanda are prime examples of being forced into change. For April, who is struggling in college, her only motivation to change is to "get her parents off her back." In addition, she is not clear on what she wants, where she wants to go after college, or what is important to her. (A good coach can help you answer all of these questions but only if you want to know the answer.) Amanda is also not clear on what she wants. She is only clear that she doesn't want to be an outsider. She is willing to change to avoid the negative consequence of being fired, but she also believes that being fired might not be enough of a negative outcome to motivate change. Sheesh.

On the flip side, Mark and Emily are shining examples of embracing change. They are both clear about what they want: Mark wants to get a job, and Emily wants to reach her sales and networking goals. They both believe that the result they are working toward will be worth the time and energy it will take to get them there.

Interestingly enough, after choosing these examples, I realized that both of the "embracing change" examples are also excellent success stories. Mark took to heart everything we discovered in just two sessions, and he was offered the very next job he interviewed for within a few weeks. Emily is now ranked in the top ten nationwide for sales within her company. These are two shining examples of Stars.

Things didn't work out so well for the two people who were forced to change—and who never found their own motivation to change. Both April and Amanda abandoned their attempts at coaching almost before they got started. April wound up taking summer school but not the extra semester. She did graduate from college but still lives with her parents and has a part-time job at the ice cream shop where she worked while in high school. She has yet to choose a career path. Amanda was fired.

G.R.E.A.T. Goal Activity 2-2

Answer the following questions:

1. Are you reading this book because you "want to" or because you feel like you're being "forced to"? (Note: Everyone will be in both categories at some point in their lives. No one is judging your motivation; you simply want to know what your dominant attitude is right now.)
2. If you are being forced to change, what needs to shift for you to embrace the change? Do you need to shift something about yourself or maybe adjust your goal so it can become a priority?
3. After you have answered the two questions above, grab your notebook and create two columns. In the first column, list

specific examples of when you have been forced to change and then write what the outcome was. Did the changes happen? In the second column, list specific examples of when you have embraced change. Again, write what the outcome was. Did the changes happen? Which column has more examples? Which column has more successes? In which column did you experience more fulfillment?

In this chapter, you learned how people are inadvertently trained from a young age to be "smart" and to make conservative and often safe choices that don't cause much risk—and for which the results are often small. You also learned the differences between being smart versus being G.R.E.A.T. We've discussed the mindset of change and how your results will vary greatly depending on whether you *want to* or you *have to* change.

You have already been challenged to complete your first two G.R.E.A.T. Goal Activities. Now I'll give you one more challenge. I highly encourage you to complete these activities before you continue to chapter 3. You'll be glad you did.

G.R.E.A.T. Goal Activity 2-3

Now you have read and understand the two main reasons that cause people to change. You have also admitted to yourself that you are ready and willing to make a change, or perhaps you were forced to change, but your reason to move forward is strong. Regardless of the original reason that put you on this path, are you ready to commit to yourself and this goal-setting process? If the answer is YES (and I hope it is), please fill out the G.R.E.A.T. Goals pledge below and then keep reading.

I, _____, pledge that I will finish reading G.R.E.A.T. Goals and complete all G.R.E.A.T. Goal Activities by _____ (date), which is no more than thirty days from now. Furthermore, I pledge to give this goal-setting process my focus and energy and make it my top priority because I believe that being G.R.E.A.T. is worth the investment.

_____   _____

Signed   Date

Three

Discovering Your Dream

Whew! You made it to chapter 3. Hopefully you finished the exercises in chapter 2 and have clarified your motivations for change. In this chapter, we will explore what you want. This can be intimidating because to admit what you really want, you have to admit how far you are from your ideal life. It's also the place you start dreaming about your ideal future, though, so stick with it. By the end of this chapter, you will have a greater understanding of what makes you feel challenged, happy, and fulfilled.

What Do You Want?

It is such a simple question yet such an important one. The answer is vital to having a fulfilled life, yet so many of us have a difficult time answering. We may be overwhelmed by the possibilities, have been trained to be demure about our wants or feel ashamed to admit our answer.

What is the course you want your life to take? You only have a finite amount of time on this planet. What do you want to accomplish with your time while you're here? What do you hope to leave behind? Who do you want to be and what legacy will you leave? I have said before that you cannot reach your destination unless you know what it is. So what *is* your destination?

What do you want?

At this point, some of you are in a panic. Maybe you have no idea what inspires you. You might know what you don't want (and this is likely what you already have), but you have no idea what you do want. Some of you may have been so focused on merely surviving that you have had to put all your desires aside, and now you can't even remember what they were. Maybe you are a person who has spent the last ten or twenty years putting other's needs and expectations before your own. This is an easy habit to get into when we are not sure what we want; we simply take other's desires and make them our own. Maybe you have taken your dreams and aspirations, packed them away in an imaginary little box, shoved them deep into the back of your mind, and there they lay, dusty and forgotten.

Why We Don't Know

Maybe you know what you want but are embarrassed by it. You might feel shame for not being grateful for what you have. After all, so many people have it worse. You worry that people will laugh if you share your desire. You fear they will think you selfish for wanting more because, to be completely honest, you feel a little selfish for wanting it. Maybe you worry that if you share your desire, really put it out there, and then don't reach it, it will mean that you have failed, or worse, that you are a failure.

It wasn't always like this. Ask any seven-year-old what he or she wants to be as a grown up, and you will get a quick answer: "I want to be a fireman…a ballerina…a doctor…a mom…president."

Sometimes it's a fantastic combination that makes no sense to our adult minds: "I want to be a sea captain/farmer...a dentist/gymnast... a police officer/cupcake maker." Or my answer at seven years old: "A one-millionaire/opera singer/cowgirl!" (In my defense, a million dollars was a lot of money back then, and I was a little horse crazy.) Kids are proud of their desires, and these answers make perfect sense to them. These are the things they love; of course they will spend their entire lives doing them. How could they not? They can't envision a world that does not allow them to be what they want to be.

Unfortunately, sometime in the next decade, these young idealists learn that they can't always have what they want. How many of you heard that from your parents when you were growing up? I know I did. Kids learn that sacrifices must be made. That some expectations must be adjusted. That compromise is a good thing.

As children, we learn not to be selfish (another of those horrid labels that most of us try like mad to avoid). We are told to be grateful for what we have. After all, "there are children starving in [fill in the blank]." We learn that what we want is not always what is smart and that being smart is more important. Sometimes, we learn that we are not worthy of our dreams.

Of course, our dreams often change as we become adults. The danger of being a police officer becomes unappealing. When we finally get aboard a boat, we get cripplingly seasick. Or maybe what we once loved no longer excites us, and we find new passions to focus on. At some point, we decide the risk is not worth the reward, so we shift our dreams.

However, in some cases we shift our dreams before we are sure what the actual risk is to reach them. We assume the path to our destination will be fraught with toil and pain, so we stop before we even get started. We shift before we even try. We change our dreams and goals, rather than changing our path or habits, because changing a goal or dream is easier.

Is life without a goal or purpose really easier? What happens when you live a life without dreams? Without goals? Without purpose? For most people that means living a life where they are often longing for more. We spend our days learning to embrace mediocrity, when in actuality we are anything but mediocre. We spend our lives yearning to be great, but not understanding what great really means.

The first step to being G.R.E.A.T. is understanding and admitting what we want.

The equation for greatness and success is simple:

$$Passion + Focus = Success$$

First, we have to identify your passion and answer this question: What do you want?

The following activities are meant for your eyes only. Give yourself permission to answer them honestly, even if you don't think your answers are possible. The point of these exercises is to discover what is important and has meaning to you. To discover the truth behind your interests, motivations, and desires, you need to get out of your comfort zone—so don't limit your dreams.

It's okay if answering these questions takes time. Don't skip ahead and say, "I'll come back to this later." These exercises are where this book and your goals intersect into something personal and deeply valuable for you. Remember, when on a journey of self-growth, you can't take short cuts.

Open your goals notebook to a clean page, and let's get started.

G.R.E.A.T. Goal Activity 3-1

1. Write about your ideal day five years from now. Describe what happens from the moment you wake up until the moment you go to bed. Be as specific as possible. Include details such

as where you are, what you are wearing, what you are eating, what you are doing, and who are you with.

Don't censor your day. Many people modify their ideal day because they don't think they can make it happen or that it's unrealistic to reach it within a five-year timeline. I am not asking you to commit to making it happen. I'm not even asking you if you think it's possible for you to create this day within five years. I am asking what your ideal day is. There are no restrictions here. You can include anything you want. Don't limit your dream.

2. Write your obituary. If you died tomorrow, how would your life be summed up? What did you accomplish? What difference did you make in the lives of others? What was your legacy? How will you be remembered?

3. Next, rewrite the obituary into your *ideal* obituary. What do you want to accomplish? What do you want your legacy to be? How do you want to be remembered? In whose life do you wish you had made a difference?

4. Now, compare your obituaries. How is your ideal different from your reality? Make sure to write down all your thoughts when you compare both versions of your obituary. This is a great exercise to capture how you truly feel about things in your life.

5. Imagine that you have found a magic lamp, and a genie has popped out and granted you three wishes. What would those wishes be? (The only rule is that you can't wish for more wishes; that's cheating.)

6. Think back to the times you were at your happiest, your most fulfilled, or your greatest. List three specific times when you were at your absolute best. Describe what you looked like when you were at your best, both physically and mentally. Also describe how you appeared to others, both physically and mentally when you were at your best.

7. Now ask three people to share when they see you at your best and what that looks like to them. Make sure to ask only the people whose opinions you trust.

8. When you were young, what did you want to be when you grew up? When did that change? What caused the change? If I asked you now (as an adult) what you want to be when you grow up, what would your answer be?

9. Create a vision board. Gather as many magazines as you can, scissors, glue, and a large piece of poster board or paper. Flip through the magazines and clip out anything that you respond to positively. Anything that you like, love, or want. Once you have gathered your pictures, add words and phrases and glue them in a montage to your poster board. When done, the poster should create an image of the things and ideas you want more of in your life. Hang your poster where you can see it every day. If you are so inclined, take a photo of it and share it with others on our G.R.E.A.T. Goals community board at eyesontheprizebook.com.

   If you would prefer to have a digital version, you can create the same idea of a vision board but instead put yours online. Many of my clients have used Pinterest to create their vision board. That way, you can keep it in your phone or on your computer and have it with you wherever you go. If you go this route instead of creating a paper version, I still recommend that you look at it often. Just as you didn't censor your ideal day, don't censor your vision board either. At this point, you don't have to worry about making this your reality; this is just to get an idea of where you want to be.

10. Set a timer for three minutes. Brainstorm everything you love or that excites you. It doesn't matter if these things seem important or not, just write down as many as you can in three

minutes. At the end of three minutes, read your list. Can you see any patterns? Are there any surprises?

11. Sometimes it's easier for people to identify what they don't want than what they do want. So here is an exercise to see if we can turn "don't wants" into "wants." Set a timer for two minutes and brainstorm a list of what you don't want. When your time is up, take a moment to look at every item and see if you can shift each one from a "don't want" into a "want." Here are a few examples:

I Don't Want	I Want
To live paycheck to paycheck	To make enough to cover necessities and have a financial surplus
To work at a desk	To work outdoors
To be bored	To be excited and passionate
To be stagnant	To be moving forward and growing

With all that you learned about yourself from answering the questions in the exercises above, this chapter has established the foundation for the G.R.E.A.T. Goals system. After you define what you want and what makes you feel happy and fulfilled, you can take the next steps toward making your dreams a reality. To get the most value out of G.R.E.A.T. Goals, make sure you complete the exercises above before you move on to the next chapter. If you are struggling with some of the questions in this chapter, consider logging onto the G.R.E.A.T. Goals community board at eyesontheprizebook.com for support through this process.

Four

Genuine

So far we've talked about goals and why they are important. The system that I have developed in this book is called G.R.E.A.T. Goals. Let's start breaking down the acronym to better understand what I mean by "G.R.E.A.T."

A G.R.E.A.T. Goal is Genuine, Reachable, Exact, Affirmative, and Totalitarian. This chapter is primarily about the importance of making your goals Genuine, the impetus of goals in our lives, and the powerful forces that motivate (or de-motivate) us all. In this chapter, we will explore the goals in your life and how to shift your perspective to get the best results, even when you are less than excited about a goal. Read on to harness the power of genuine goal setting and to produce excellent results.

G = Genuine
To make a goal G.R.E.A.T., it must be *genuine* for you. That means it must be both self-motivated and desirable. Sounds simple, right? Why

would we bother to set a goal if we didn't want to reach it? However, reality is not always so simple. There are many times in life when the goals we are striving to achieve have been given to us, or forced upon us by others. Take, for example, children whose parent insists they get good grades, or the salespeople who are expected to hit a certain sales quota each month, or the managers who are assigned projects they don't want with teams they did not choose. It is not uncommon for an outside influence to assign goals and benchmarks to our personal performances.

Which do you think would have better results? Goals you want to achieve or goals someone else said you *must* achieve?

Controlled versus Autonomous Goals

There are two main platforms of motivation when it comes to goals: *controlled* and *autonomous*. **Controlled goals** are goals that are less self-motivated and have usually been given or assigned to you by an outside source. Controlled goals can be broken down into two subtypes: *external* and *introjected*.

External: "You have to"
Introjected: "I should"

External goals are outer-motivated, those given to you by an outside source such as a parent, a boss, a spouse, or a teacher. You have little to no say in the broad scope of the goal (i.e., what you need to accomplish) or the specifics of the goal, like the timeline, the measures of success, even the tools needed to reach the goal. External goals are just that: external influences projecting their goals onto your performance. They are communicated to you by others telling you what they want you to do and require you to fulfill their expectations of what your performance and success should be. This type of goal can often result in making you feel helpless, resentful, and unmotivated.

One step further is the introjected goal. Introjection is the opposite of projection; these are goals you force upon yourself. Introjected goals are technically self-motivated because you choose them, but you choose them because you feel obligated, forced, or expected to do so. These are the things you feel you have to do, or you should do, but you don't necessarily want to do. For example, a child might feel obligated to get an A in a subject because an older sibling achieved this. The expectation may not have been explicitly stated to the child, but the pressure is still felt, whether or not his or her interests or skill sets are similar to those of the sibling. Introjected goals often sound like "I should" in our heads and are often accompanied by a sense of resistance, frustration, or failure, whether we have failed or not.

The other platform for motivation is the autonomous goal.

Autonomous goals are desirable to the goal setter and completely self-motivated. You choose to create these goals because you love the process, or you honestly want to challenge yourself to reach the achievement you have set for yourself. You already believe that the risk and effort is worth the reward.

Autonomous goals can also be broken down into two subtypes: *intrinsic* and *identified*.

Intrinsic: "For the love of something I'm passionate about"
Identified: "I truly want to try something new"

Intrinsic goals are marked by a true passion for what you are trying to achieve or the process used to achieve it. The interest or enjoyment comes from the task itself and exists within the individual rather than relying on external pressures or a desire for reward. For example, the salespeople who exceed their quota because they love the product, or the students who ace the test because they love the subject. These are both examples of success that is driven from a personal passion unique to an interest or skill set. Usually, an intrinsic goal is related to something you have already tried or accomplished or a skill you have already mastered, and you enjoyed or loved the experience.

Identified goals are different from intrinsic goals because, while you want the experience and to achieve the goal, you don't have the certainty that you love the process or the results. Identified goals are usually goals that are outside your current skill level or comfort zone. You have never done it or had it, but you know you want it. For example, say you're a nonrunner, and you set a goal to train for and finish a 5K run. For you, the goal is identified. You know you want to reach your goal, but it is a new experience and process for you. However, if you love running, or you have already had a fantastic experience finishing a 5K and you set the exact same goal, it becomes intrinsic. The same goal can either be intrinsic or identified based on your perspective and prior experience.

Controlled versus Autonomous Goals

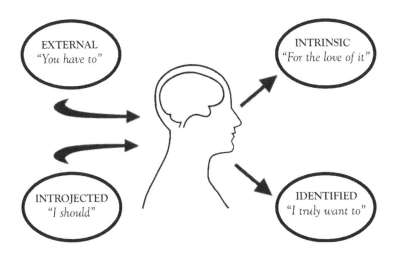

I'm sure it's no surprise to you that, statistically speaking, the majority of people striving to reach controlled goals will fail. You are much more likely to achieve an autonomous goal, one that is self-motivated. In fact, one study suggests that you are up to 80 percent more likely to reach an autonomous goal as opposed to a controlled goal. A 2010 study regarding controlled versus autonomous goals for students found further proof that autonomous goals were associated with positive outcomes such as increased concentration, persistence, time management, and deep learning. In contrast, controlled motivation had predictable negative outcomes such as maladaptive coping strategies, test anxiety, superficial learning, and school dropout. These results were obtained across age groups (i.e., from elementary to high school) and across cultures (e.g., Belgium, Canada, China, Japan, Russia, and the United States).

If your goal is to go back to school to further your education, but you feel forced to go, you will find many excuses as to why you can't do this. Large obstacles will suddenly appear and your motivation will be lacking. However, if your personal reasons for going back to school are strong enough, almost nothing can stop you from achieving your goal. Let's take a look at the state of obesity in the United States. According to the Center for Disease Control, over 36 percent of the United States population is currently obese, and the Organization for Economic Cooperation predicts that by the year 2020, 75 percent of our country will be overweight or obese. We know that being overweight or obese can have a catastrophic influence on our health, with increasing rates of heart attacks, high blood pressure, stroke, diabetes, and cancer to name a few. Doctors consistently warn their patients of the dangers of being overweight and encourage their patients to lose weight, yet the obesity rate keeps growing.

It's not like the American public doesn't try. The diet industry is a $60 billion-plus industry; an estimated 45 million Americans diet every year. So why are we getting heavier? I think it's in the nature of the reason behind setting a weight-loss goal. We do it because the doctor said to or because we should in order to be healthier. Notice that both of those reasons are controlled and not autonomous. The goal is forced upon us from a source outside ourselves.

What does all this mean? **If you want it, you will work for it. If you don't, you won't.** So in order to make sure your goal is G.R.E.A.T., we need to make sure you really want it. To maximize your motivation and give you a greater chance of statistical success, regardless of how this goal began for you, we need to make sure that, your goal is autonomous rather than controlled.

Below is a set of activities designed to help you identify and understand the motivation behind your goal. You can complete this section multiple times for each goal you may have. Make sure that you take the time to jot down your answers to the questions before proceeding as this is an idea-generating exercise that will set the groundwork to help you get the most benefit when you read the next few chapters.

G.R.E.A.T. Goal Activity 4-1

1. What is your goal? (This can be a very rough version for now; it doesn't need to be perfect. You will refine it throughout the next few chapters. At this point, simply write down what you want).
2. Who will be the happiest if you reach this goal? You, your parent, your spouse, your boss, or someone else?
3. What will change in your life when you have reached this goal? List all the things you will gain and all the things you will lose.
4. On a scale of one to one hundred (one being not at all, one hundred being "I will do whatever it takes"), how much do you want to reach this goal?

5. Is this goal controlled (does someone expect you to make this change) or autonomous (did you set the goal for yourself)? If it is controlled, is it external ("I have to") or introjected ("I should")? If it is autonomous, is it intrinsic ("I've already tried this, and I loved the experience") or identified ("I've never done this, but I know I want to")? How do you know which type of goal you have? If you're not sure, here is one example modified for each combination to help you decide.

Goal: To try out for the basketball team.

- If your goal is controlled and introjected, your motivation might be to try out because your parents said, "You have to."

- If your goal is controlled and external, your motivation might be to try out because colleges look for extracurricular activities. You want to go to a good college, so you "should" try out.

- On the other hand, if your goal is autonomous and intrinsic, your motivation might be that you love basketball and want to play every chance you get.

- Finally, if your goal is autonomous and identified, your motivation might be to try out because you want to challenge your basketball skills and see how you compare.

The benefit to knowing the factors that are shaping your situation is that you can more quickly identify what you need to shift so the outcome of your goal is positive.

Shifting Your Motivation

Now that you can see your goal more clearly, let's begin to expand your choices. If your goal is controlled because someone else is expecting you to change something, all is not lost. You are not doomed to fail. However, if you want to increase the probability that you will reach your goal, you need to shift your controlled goal to an autonomous goal. "How is this possible?" you may ask. "There is no way I am ever going to want to do _____."

You can shift your goal from controlled to autonomous in two ways:

1. Tie the achievement of the goal to an achievement or reward that is valuable to you.
2. Create a goal that aligns with your values and wants, which will not-so-coincidentally also result in the achievement of the controlled goal.

It is fairly simple to tie the achievement of a goal to a reward system. For example, I had a client named Addison who was told by her doctor that she needed to lose fifty pounds. She was prediabetic, prehypertensive, and had a chronic knee injury. There were obvious health benefits to losing the weight. Yet Addison had issues with the idea of being "forced" to lose weight. As a result, she had been losing and gaining the same seven pounds for months. Addison was also an avid traveler. She loved nothing more than traveling to new places, seeing new things, and meeting new people. So she came up with a fitness and travel-based reward system for weight loss. She chose target milestones of weight loss and came up with a prize for each one. At fifteen pounds she earned a weekend in the mountains with a day of hiking. At thirty pounds she earned a weekend at the beach and a surfing lesson. At fifty pounds she earned a walking trip through Spain. This final trip was a culmination of her achievement—she had dreamed of going but had never been able to because she couldn't walk the five to ten miles a day required.

This is a simple and effective strategy to reach an immediate goal, but note that your motivation will only be as strong as your desire to earn the reward. The value of the reward must be worth more than the effort it takes to earn it, or it is too easy to cut and run when the process gets difficult. If you choose this method, make sure the reward is motivating enough and that this method is sustainable—that you can keep your promise to follow through on providing the reward.

The second technique to achieve a controlled goal, through aligning your values and wants, requires a bit more thought. To make it work, you have to find your own reason to take action that will result in achieving the goal. For example, Randy's boss required that he bring in twenty new customers a month. Randy hated the hard sell and resented the fact that reaching a new customer quota was required to be his priority. Randy, however, did love networking and meeting new people. When he looked at his numbers, he learned that for every one hundred people he connected with outside of work at networking or business events, roughly twenty of them became his customers. So by shifting his goal to "I will meet one hundred new people per month at business and networking events," he knew that a residual result of that action would be reaching the dictated quota of twenty new customers a month.

Just as a side note, a reward-based system can help motivate you to achieve a specific goal. A realignment of values can help you *exceed* a goal. From the examples above, Addison lost her fifty pounds, but Randy, who used his enjoyment of meeting people to motivate himself, ended up meeting an average of two hundred new people a month. As a result, Randy consistently came in over quota and was named salesperson of the month eight months in a row! When you can identify a core value or desire inside of a controlled goal, and harness that as your motivation, you are making the quantum leap from "should" and "have to" into "want to" and "for the love of it."

If your goal is already intrinsic or identified, meaning that you set the goal and it's something either somewhat familiar or its new and you're excited to get started, good for you! You are on your way to your G.R.E.A.T. Goal. If not, don't fear. We simply need to shift your controlled goal and make it autonomous. The activity below will help you begin.

G.R.E.A.T. Goal Activity 4-2

1. Identify any controlled goals in your list from Activity 4-1 earlier in the chapter.
2. Brainstorm whether each goal can be shifted by restating the goal into something you will enjoy achieving or by tying a reward to the achievement of a goal.

In this chapter, you learned that a goal must be Genuine. You must be motivated to achieve it based on your own enthusiasm. So whether you set your goal or it was urged upon you by outside circumstances, now you have clarity about how to move forward and be successful. We explored this by looking at the differences between autonomous goals versus controlled goals. When you are motivated to make a change, you will work toward your goal. If you aren't motivated, you won't work toward it. You learned that autonomous goals have a greater chance of success but that you can convert controlled goals into autonomous goals to improve the odds that you'll be successful. You identified your personal goals as autonomous or controlled and brainstormed ways to shift your goals to make them more achievable. Make sure you complete all your activities before continuing to chapter 5, Reachable.

Five

This chapter is about creating Reachable goals. To be clear, this chapter is not about squashing your big dreams or modifying your goal to make it more attainable. It is simply encouraging you to make your goal realistic and reachable. You have the potential to make your dreams your reality. This chapter is a reminder that it takes effort and focus to achieve your dreams—not just desire.

R = Reachable

Ask yourself if your goal is reachable given the amount of time and effort you are willing to put into it. If you give it your all, can you attain it? A G.R.E.A.T Goal should be challenging. It should stretch you to or beyond the limits of your ability, but it must also be possible. It should require work, effort, learning, and growth to make it happen. But if you can't realistically reach your goal, you won't bother to give it your all.

A reachable goal is all about attitude and perspective. Do you believe it is possible? Are you willing to put in the time and effort necessary to get there? Are you willing to do whatever it takes to make your goal reality? To set a successful goal, you will need to both believe you can achieve it and commit your time, energy, and resources to its completion.

Staying motivated is one of the biggest issues my clients struggle with. I can't tell you how often clients share large, ambitious goals with tight deadlines. These are goals that will stretch them to their limits and will take everything they have to reach. And then in the next sentence, they will tell me they can really only dedicate fifteen minutes a day to this project because they are so incredibly busy and overwhelmed. There is no way they can achieve their goals in the timeline or with the resources they have stated unless they are willing to dedicate more time and energy to the project. They have set goals that ensure failure because they are unreachable given the time and effort they are willing to dedicate to the process.

What would happen if a candidate for the office of president of the United States said, "I really want to be president, but I only have an hour a day to commit to my campaign." Do you think he or she would win? Would voters even take that candidate seriously? More importantly, is that candidate taking running for president seriously?

How about if someone who has never picked up a violin suddenly decides to be a concert violinist? Possible, right? With years of hard work, hundreds of lessons, and endless hours of practice, that goal can be reached. What if the goal is to be a concert violinist in one year? Suddenly this goal is less probable. It could still happen if every waking moment is dedicated to practicing the violin, but the goal has become less doable, less reachable.

What if this person said, "I really want to be a concert violinist in one year. Oh, and I only have time to practice once a week." Suddenly the goal goes from probable, to possible, to impossible. This is what happens when you set an unreachable goal.

When a goal is not reachable, we are less likely to give it 100 percent of our effort. Deep down we realize that even if we give it 100 percent, we still won't be able to reach it, so what's the point? So if a goal is unreachable, you essentially stop trying, because why bother to try if you can't succeed?

Keeping It Realistic

One final example of a goal that has been made unreachable (and I have been guilty of this one myself): "I want to lose twenty pounds in three months." This is an achievable goal assuming you have twenty pounds to lose, right? The timeline seems ambitious but not impossible. At first glance this goal seems achievable. What if instead the person said, "I want to lose twenty pounds in three months, and I don't want to modify my diet in any way." Suddenly it is a bit harder to reach the goal. It is still possible with lots of exercise, but it is less likely this person can achieve the desired results. What if the person who wants to lose weight said, "I want to lose twenty pounds in three months. I don't want to modify my diet in any way, and I only have an hour a day, three days a week to work out." What just happened to the reachability factor of this goal? It went from a ten (totally achievable) to a one (practically impossible). There is a Quotient of Reachability in terms of goal setting: the more focus, time, energy, and resources you give to reaching a goal, the more likely it is that you will achieve that goal. The more limitations you place on the focus, time, energy, and resources you are willing to dedicate, the less likely success becomes. An obtainable weight loss goal becomes unobtainable once reachability quotient is ignored.

Reachability Factor

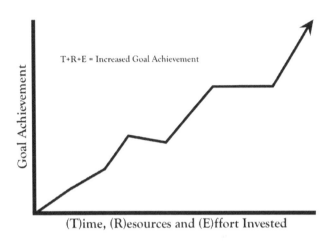

T+R+E = Increased Goal Achievement

Goal Achievement

(T)ime, (R)esources and (E)ffort Invested

Don't mistake a reachable goal for an easy goal or make the mistake of thinking that you have to limit your dreams and goals to make them reachable. Set a big, audacious, life-changing goal for yourself and be willing to dedicate the focus, time, energy, and resources it will take to reach that goal. As we mentioned before, a G.R.E.A.T. Goal is one that pushes you to grow. A G.R.E.A.T. Goal should be outside of your comfort zone—the certainty of reaching it shouldn't be 100 percent. But you do have to know that it is possible for you to reach that goal, and you do have to be willing to put in the work.

If you don't believe you can reach your goal, you can't reach it. You must be willing to make your goal a priority, dedicate time and energy to it, and take focused action—otherwise your goal will stay a dream, never becoming your reality.

G.R.E.A.T. Goal Activity 5-1

1. List three goals you have set and reached in the past. Did you know you would reach them when you started?
2. List three goals you set and did not reach. Were they reachable goals? Why or why not?
3. List three goals that you daydream about accomplishing but that you believe are unreachable. What makes them unreachable? Is there a way to shift them to become reachable?

Commitment

There are two things I want you to remember about making your goal reachable. First, if you believe it is possible, it is. Conversely, if you believe it is impossible, it is. This is along the lines of that old Henry Ford saying, "Whether you think you can, or you think you can't—you're right." Your perception of the feasibility of a goal can dictate the ultimate result. Remember the story of *The Little Engine That Could* from your childhood? The train made it to the top of the mountain with the engine saying, "I think I can, I think I can, I think I can." What would have happened if instead he said, "I know I can't"?

Second, remember that people who are committed to reaching their goals—by making it a priority and dedicating time and energy to it—are more likely to succeed. The probability that you will reach your goal is directly related to how committed you are to reaching it. Remember, to reach your G.R.E.A.T. Goal, you will need to both believe you can achieve it and commit your time, energy, and resources to its completion.

So with that in mind, let's take a moment to explore your commitment.

G.R.E.A.T. Goal Activity 5-2

1. Brainstorm the qualities and actions of a committed goal setter (e.g., showing up on time). I've provided a list below to get you started. Add your qualities to the list.
2. How many of these qualities and actions do you currently possess and express?
3. Which qualities and actions would you like to possess and express?
4. What is the one thing you can do today to gain one of those qualities?

Qualities and Actions of Dedicated Goal Setters
Keep their word
Make their commitments a priority
Delegate specific time to their commitments
Are consistent
Are persistent
Are flexible
Don't make excuses
Look at obstacles as challenges rather than reasons to stop
Plan ahead
Don't quit
Believe things are possible

5. Now let's take a look at your goal.
   a. Is it a challenge? Will it take effort and drive to attain it? We want to be sure you have not made your goal reachable simply by making it easy to achieve.

b. Is there a timeline or due date to this goal? (We will talk more about adding a timeline in the next chapter.) Is the timeline challenging yet possible?

c. Look at your schedule realistically. How much time can you dedicate to reaching this goal?

d. On a blank sheet of paper, draw a circle or go to our website (eyesontheprizebook.com) and print out our Circle of Time Worksheet. Using colored pencils, shade in how you spend your time during any given day. Each pie piece represents one hour. Here are the mandatory activities you must include: sleeping, eating and food prep, work, commute/travel time, grooming/hygiene, cleaning/chores. The rest of your chart should include whatever else you do. Here are some ideas: exercising, Internet, TV, reading, socializing, school, studying, writing, networking, hobbies, volunteering, childcare. Each activity should be filled in using a different color.

How much of your day is left to dedicate to your goal?

Some people work better on a weekly basis because their day-to-day routine varies radically. Others work better if they have a specific daily schedule. There are 168 hours in a week. Using your colored pencils and a color key, create and fill out a weekly time chart (or use the version available on our website eyesontheprizebook.com). Each square = one hour.

1. How many extra hours a week do you have available to dedicate to your goal?

2. Is there something on your schedule that you can move, reduce, or eliminate to give your goal more time? What and how?

3. Is your goal reachable? Why or why not? If not, what needs to shift to make it reachable: you or the goal?

In this chapter, we discussed how attitude and perception are critical in shaping a G.R.E.A.T. Goal. Hopefully you have created a goal that is reachable as well as a challenge to achieve. There were a hefty number of G.R.E.A.T. Goal Activities. If you haven't done all of them, take the time now to go back and do those you may have skipped. If you did them all, you should feel more clarified about the time and energy you have available to commit to your goal.

Six

Exact

So far we have learned that a G.R.E.A.T. Goal must be Genuine and Reachable. In this chapter, we will be discussing the importance of having an Exact goal. An exact goal will not only define what success means to you, but it will give you a definitive finish line—a point where you know you have succeeded and you can celebrate. Read on to learn how to make your goal exact.

E = Exact

A G.R.E.A.T. Goal is as exact and specific as possible. You should always know the who, what, when, and where of your goal when you set it. Eventually you need to know the how and the why, but we will focus on that in a later chapter. For now, we will focus on the 5Ws.

1. **Who** will be achieving this goal? (This is a trick question. It should always be you.)
2. **What** is the goal?

3. **W**hen is the deadline, or how much time are you devoting?
4. **W**here will this happen?
5. **W**hy do you want to achieve your goal? (You should have the answer to this from chapter 4, Genuine.)

There are a few additional specifics that you should have the answers to eventually. You don't have to include these in the phrasing of your goal, but you should keep them in the back of your mind:

1. How are you going to get there?
2. What method and tools do you need? (We will discuss this more in depth in chapter 9.)

When you phrase your goal, it will always include who, what, and when. If there is a specific where, include that as well. For example, if your goal is to run a marathon, state which one and that will give you the when and where. Why and how can be included in your phrasing if you choose to, although it is not necessary. However, you must know these answers before you can reach your goal.

Paint a Picture

Visualize all the details of completing your goal and especially make sure the end point is solid and well established. Instead of "I want to lose weight," try "I want to go from my current weight of 163 pounds to 140 pounds before November 28." Instead of "I want to make more money," try "I want to net an extra $500 a month by taking on freelance web design projects." A clear, nonambiguous, measurable goal is easier to obtain than a generalized goal that's open to interpretation.

Don't fall into the trap of using perfection language when setting your goal. Avoid words like best, more, better. Steer clear of adjectives and rely on nouns and verbs. For example, instead of saying, "I want to be a better mom," say "I want to be a mom who consistently makes the growth, health, and happiness of her children a priority." We removed the adjective "better" from the first statement and used action words and nouns to describe what we mean by better. Another reason for this is when you rely on ambiguous terms like "more" and "better," you tend to push the goal outward—and never achieve it. Let's go back to the example "I want to make more money." If you don't quantify how much more and add a timeframe to boot, you've put yourself on a hamster wheel of perpetual dissatisfaction. How much more do you have to achieve until you can check that goal off your list?

There's an element of denial in making a goal so ambiguous you can never achieve it—an element of not being kind to yourself, never allowing yourself the satisfaction of a job well done. Conversely, there's also an element of not being accountable when you don't paint a clear picture of a goal's endpoint.

The whole process can get muddied up and potentially abandoned due to lack of vision. Be crystal clear about when your goal is reached. Know where your finish line is so you'll know exactly when you've crossed it and can celebrate accordingly.

G.R.E.A.T. Goal Activity 6-1

Read the following five examples of goals. For each example, list the who, what, when, and where. If the goal is missing who, what, when, or where, rewrite the goal so that it is complete. If the example goal is missing a *why*, try to supply one.

Example:
Goal: I will run the entire Rock 'n' Roll Half Marathon in Los Angeles on October 29.

- Who: I
- What: Will run the entire half marathon.
- When: October 29
- Where: Los Angeles, CA
- Why: To get fit. To prove I can.
  1. Goal: I will be a better boss.
  2. Goal: I will finish writing my novel.
  3. Goal: I will support myself with my acting.
  4. Goal: I will earn $100,000 this year.
  5. Goal: I will lose fifty pounds.

Why is being exact and detailed important? For two simple reasons:

1. The more specific the goal, the easier it is to know when you have crossed the finish line. If a goal is vague or uncertain, it is difficult to tell exactly when you have achieved it. You need to know where your finish line is. That way you can celebrate when you cross it.

2. You need to know what is expected of you as specifically as possible so that you can plan and pace yourself. If you have no idea how long your journey will take, you can't accurately plan ahead. There is nothing worse than thinking you are running a 5K, only to find out that you have signed up for a half marathon. Proper planning and pacing is what increases your odds of accomplishing your goal.

Here is an example I like to use: Say you get a call from your friend, and he or she leaves a message saying "Hey, I'm in town this weekend. We should get together." That's all the information you are given, and you have no way of contacting your friend. Pretend you both don't have cell phones. What are the odds that you will get together this weekend? Practically zero, right?

What if instead your friend said, "Hey, I'm in town this weekend. We should get together. Let's meet at the northeast corner of Hollywood and Highland at 8:00 p.m. on Friday. We can go out to dinner."

Now what are the odds you will get together? Much greater, right? You know when and where you are expected to meet. You even know what you will be doing. You have all the expectations and parameters required for you to meet your goal, and because your friend has been exact, it's easy for you to accomplish your goal of getting together.

This is what happens when you set an exact and detailed goal. It actually becomes easier to achieve because you know what is expected and you can plan accordingly. Your chance of success grows exponentially.

G.R.E.A.T. Goal Activity 6-2

1. Examine your goals to see how specific they are.
2. Answer each of the 5W questions for your goal: who, what, when, where, and why. This is the formula for capturing a complete description of your goal since none of these questions can be answered with a simple yes or no. Who will accomplish this goal? What is the goal? When is your deadline to complete this goal? Where will this goal happen? Why is achieving this goal important to me?

In this chapter, we reviewed how to make your goal as exact as possible using the 5Ws: who, what, when, where, and why. By using these questions to fully define your goal, you will not only have all the tools you need to visualize your success but you will also know definitively when you have achieved it. Once you have completed the activities in this chapter, you are ready to move on to chapter 7, where we will explore the power of affirmative goal setting.

Seven

To achieve a goal, you must keep it in the forefront of your mind. Your goal must become such a priority for you that you repeat it to yourself several times a day. For this reason, how you approach and phrase your goals is incredibly important. This chapter will help you understand what approach and avoidance goals are and how different types of motivation impact the likelihood of your success. Read more in this chapter about affirmative goal setting and proper goal phrasing for optimal results.

A = Affirmative

When I'm working with clients who are in the goal-setting phase of the coaching process, I encourage them to make their goals as affirmative in nature as possible. This is done both in the action of the goal itself as well as in the phrasing of the goal.

In coaching we don't necessarily categorize a goal as essentially positive or negative, but we do differentiate between *approach goals* and *avoidance goals*.

Approach goals are when you are working to attain, achieve, or gain something. Usually the goal is working toward something. Here are a few examples:

1. I want to run a marathon.
2. I want to graduate from college.
3. I want to make a million dollars.
4. I want to buy a house.
5. I want to take a trip.

By contrast, avoidance goals are when you are working to stop, limit, or remove something. Usually, the goal is to avoid the consequences of an outcome. Here are a few examples:

1. I want to quit smoking.
2. I want to stop biting my nails.
3. I want to lose weight.
4. I want to stop procrastinating.
5. I want to avoid divorce.

Approach versus Avoidance Goals

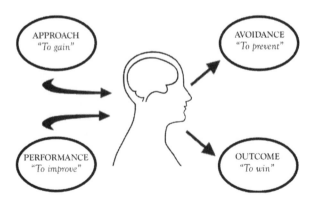

Both types of goals are achievable, but when you write goals from a more positive perspective, your outcome is more likely to be successful. Why are approach goals so important? Simply put, we are psychologically programmed to work toward gaining something rather than avoiding something. Approach goals are easier to assess when it comes to progress. If you are working to achieve something, it's easier to measure how far you have come and how far you have yet to go. Approach goals are also considered more manageable than avoidance goals, and achieving them makes you feel good.

Approach goals will make you feel more positive. When working toward an approach goal, you are focused on monitoring your own positive outcomes. You are focused almost entirely on growth and progress. There is also a great potential side effect of focusing on the positive: you can actually increase your Positivity Ratio. Barbara L. Frederickson, PhD, an author and leading scholar in the field of positive psychology, believes that increasing the amount of positivity you experience over time can actually increase your Positivity Ratio. Your Positivity Ratio is the amount of positive emotions you experience divided by the amount of negative emotions you experience in the same period of time. A low Positivity Ratio can lead to a languishing downward spiral of emotion and productivity. Conversely, a high Positivity Ratio can spiral upward, prompting increases in joy, productivity, and creativity. The tipping point between low and high seems to be 3:1.

By contrast, avoidance goals require monitoring negative outcomes, and the tiniest slip can mean failure. Studies have shown that focusing on negatives over time can actually cause you mental and physical stress, thus creating anxiety and extra hurdles as you pursue your goal.

Have you ever felt your heart race or your body tense after being told no? According to a study published by psychologytoday.com, if we were monitoring your brain in an MRI machine and flashed the word no for less than one second, we'd suddenly see a release of dozens of stress-producing hormones and neurotransmitters. These chemicals are responsible for interrupting the normal functions of your brain like impairing logic, reason, language processing, and communication.

This means that consistently focusing on an avoidance goal, a goal where you are measuring the negative and consistently telling yourself no, can actually increase your stress levels and reduce the likelihood that you will achieve the goal.

Here is an example of the differences between the two types of goals. The goal "I want to run a marathon" requires months of training to achieve. This is measureable, has milestones you can set, and has accomplishments you can reach almost every single day. You can consistently measure your gains and progress and monitor your improvement. However, the goal "I want to lose weight" requires constant monitoring of calorie intake versus calories burned. You must avoid foods that are bad for you, even though they taste good. You must deny your cravings and often ignore your body when it tells you it is hungry. This can leave you filled with anxiety and fear of failure. If your ultimate goal is to get healthy, which is what both of the above goals are designed to do, how you phrase and set your goal can make all the difference.

Approach goals are associated with higher perceptions of success in the task and with higher levels of satisfaction. **You are more motivated if you are working toward something desirable rather than away from something undesirable.** Simply put, when people work toward approach goals, they are more likely to reach their goals and to be happier during the process.

G.R.E.A.T. Goal Activity 7-1

1. Take the five examples of avoidance goals at the beginning of this chapter and see if you can do a quick rewrite to shift them so they become approach goals instead. If you are having difficulty, ask yourself what is trying to be gained by achieving the avoidance goal.
    a. Example: "I want to avoid divorce" can be shifted to "I want to feel happy when I'm with my partner."
    b. Example: "I want to stop procrastinating" can be shifted to "I want to consistently be prepared."
    c. Example: "I want to quit smoking" can be shifted to "I want to have happy, healthy lungs."
2. Make a list of five goals you have reached and five goals you set but did not reach. Determine if they were approach or avoidance. If they were avoidance, see if you can shift the way you phrase them so that they become approach goals.
3. Look at your primary goal. Is it approach or avoidance? Shift it so that it is an approach goal.

Rephrasing Goals for Optimal Outcomes

You just learned that when you write goals from a more positive perspective, your outcome is more likely to be successful. The second way to keep your goal affirmative in nature is to phrase it in a confident and positive way. What do I mean by this? Positively phrased goals start with *I will, I am,* or *I have,* while negative phrases start with *I want, I hope,* or *I'll try.*

Not only does a negatively phrased goal cause stress and reduce the likelihood of success, it can also undermine and potentially kill your motivation and self-confidence. Negative phrasing leaves room for doubt and uncertainty to creep in. Too much doubt and uncertainty can undermine your self-confidence and stop your momentum in its tracks. Until this point in the book, I have purposely phrased all my example goals using negative phrasing since that is what my clients tend to use at the beginning of the goal setting process. From here forward we will use affirmative phrasing.

Studies have shown that for every negative thought we have, it takes three to five positive thoughts to counteract the increased stress and decreased motivation and self-confidence caused by the negative thought. You need an abundance of self-confidence and motivation to reach your goal. That's why I encourage my clients to remind themselves of their goals multiple times a day. By doing this, they keep their goals at the forefront of their minds.

But what if the goal you repeat and remind yourself of every day, multiple times a day, is an avoidance goal? Can you imagine the damage just thinking about that goal might cause? To make matters worse, negative thinking is self-perpetuating; so the more you practice thinking negative thoughts or focusing on negative goals, the more difficult it becomes to stop that pattern and shift the negative momentum. However, when people consistently practice turning negative thoughts and worries into positive affirmations, there is a noticeable increase in confidence and self-control. By phrasing your approach goal in a positive manner, you are actually subconsciously building your self-control and confidence, which will, in turn, improve your chance of success.

Making sure your goals are phrased in an affirmative and positive way is simple:

1. Use phrases like *I will, I am,* or *I have* rather than *I want, I hope,* or *I'll try.*
2. Make sure the goal is about what you want, not what you don't want.

Just listen to the difference positive phrasing can make. Repeat the following goal out loud:

"I hope to make a million dollars." How does that phrase make you feel? When you said it out loud, did you notice your body shrug, your head tilt, or your eyebrows raise? Did you feel something in your body shift? All these responses are common signs of uncertainty that are often found with negatively phrased statements. Now repeat this goal out loud: "I will make a million dollars." Do you hear and feel the difference? If you are like most people, you reacted to the positive phrasing in this goal by lowering the tone of your voice and standing or sitting squarely, both signs of confidence.

G.R.E.A.T. Goal Activity 7-2

1. Take the five approach goals listed at the beginning of this chapter, and take the five avoidance goals you shifted into approach goals in G.R.E.A.T. Goal Activity 7-1, and make sure all ten are phrased in an affirmative nature.
2. Take the list of five goals you reached and five goals you set but did not reach from the second question in G.R.E.A.T. Goal Activity 7-1. Make a note of which were approach goals and phrased affirmatively and which were avoidance goals and phrased negatively. Is there any correlation between approach and affirmative and success for you?

3. Take your primary goal and phrase it in an affirmative nature, if you haven't already.

How did it go? This chapter helped you understand approach and avoidance goals and how different types of motivation can impact your likelihood of success. You have created your optimal goal phrasing by rewriting your goals in positive and affirmative ways, so take a breath and congratulate yourself. These aren't easy tasks to accomplish.

Eight

Totalitarian

A G.R.E.A.T. Goal so far has been Genuine, Reachable, Exact, and Affirmative. The final letter of the G.R.E.A.T. Goal stands for Totalitarian. Now I know this is a word that elicits visions of dystopian societies and power-hungry dictators, but fear not. In this context, totalitarian is a fancy word for setting goals in which you have 100 percent control over the outcome. You have absolute power to achieve them. It's about setting goals that can be measured by your efforts alone. Read more to understand how setting a totalitarian goal is important to your overall success.

T = Totalitarian

According to the Merriam-Webster Dictionary, totalitarian means: "Of or relating to centralized control by an autocratic leader (one who has undisputed influence or power) or hierarchy."

Before I go any further, let me clarify. I'm not asking you to be a goal tyrant. Nor am I saying that reaching this goal should be the only focus of your life. I am saying for a goal to be truly great, it has to be a goal that you—and only you—can make happen. The outcome should depend solely on your efforts and achievements. In the process of reaching your goal, you may need to ask for help or rely on others for education or advice, but you can't depend on anyone else to reach this goal for you. Repeat the mantra of a G.R.E.A.T. goal achiever: your goal, your effort, your success.

Often a client will come to me with a goal that they can't control:

"I want to fall in love and get married."
"I want to book my next audition."
"I want to win my next half marathon."
"I want to win the lottery."

Okay, I have never had a client come to me with the intent of reaching that last goal, but I have heard plenty of people say it. What flaw do all these goals have in common? An astute reader from the previous chapter would point out that each statement begins with "I want," which we learned in the last chapter is not affirmative enough for a G.R.E.A.T. Goal. This is true. In addition, these goals all require the efforts and decisions of someone else or something outside of the goal setter's control to reach them.

You can't fall in love and get married by yourself. It depends on someone being willing to marry you—he or she has control in the ultimate fulfillment of this goal. You do not determine if you will book the next audition. You could be brilliant and amazing, but ultimately, it's the casting agent's call. In order for you to win your next half marathon, not only do you need to train and run the best race you can, you must also depend on every other runner to be slightly slower than you. You could shave five minutes off your time and set a new personal record, but if someone happens to run faster during the race, you still fail according to your goal. And as for the lottery, need I say it? You have no control in reaching this goal. It depends on hope and chance, and unfortunately hope and chance rarely lead to success.

Hope and chance are the stuff of dreams, not of goals.

Outcome, Performance, and Process

When we categorize goals based on effort and control, we can break them into two categories: *outcome* and *performance and process*.

Outcome goals depend on the result of a competition (i.e., a race, a sporting event, a promotion, a title, getting a job). Outcome goals are only partly under the control of the goal setter and are partly dependent on other people, including but not limited to bosses, teammates, opponents, and officials. These goals depend not only on your own efforts and skills but also on those of your opponent. You can produce the best results of your life and still lose if your opponent does better than you do.

Performance and process goals are focused on achieving standards or performance objectives independently of other competitors, usually on the basis of comparisons with your own previous performances. The purpose of a performance goal is to improve your level of personal performance at a task, and it is relatively independent of the actions of others. Some people refer to performance goals as improvement goals. A process goal focuses on the action or habit that is needed to reach a goal.

Here are examples to illustrate the three types of goals:

1. Outcome: To win the pie-eating contest.
2. Performance: To eat at least one more pie than I did in my last contest.
3. Process: To practice pie eating three times a week until the contest.

G.R.E.A.T. Goal Activity 8-1

1. Determine if the following goals are outcome goals (they depend on the result of a competition) or performance goals (they depend on your personal performance).
   a. I will run a 5K next month in under thirty minutes.
   b. I will complete the "Couch to 5K" running program and run a 5K next month.
   c. I will win my age bracket in the 5K next month.
   d. I will be the top sales employee next month.
   e. I will increase my sales by 50 percent next month.
   f. I will write and publish a best seller within the next two years.
   g. I will earn $1,000,000.
   h. I will get married.
2. Look at the list of goals above. Find the goals that you labeled as outcome goals and add to or change them so they become performance goals.

Most people set only outcome goals, so don't panic if you have realized that your goal is an outcome goal. The problem is that you can't control the achievement or result. Goals based on only the outcome are extremely vulnerable to failure due to circumstances beyond your control.

With the right circumstances, it is clearly possible to achieve performance, process, or outcome goals. Why are performance and process goals more effective than outcome goals? Well, performance and process goals help boost your motivation. Your motivation is key to achieving your goal. What happens to your motivation if you work hard and do everything right, only to lose out on your goal at the very end because someone happened to have a better result? The next time you might not work as hard or as long because a little voice might be whispering, "What's the point if none of my effort matters in the end anyway?"

In addition, performance and process goals make it easier to measure progress along the way. You can measure the effort that you put into your work as well as the results of that effort. For example, you can measure not only how many times you run per week (process) you can also see results in endurance, speed, and health benefits (performance).

Finally, performance and process goals help you create a plan you can achieve. Performance goals set forth clear and defined criteria to achieve. You have control over each step of the process as you progress toward achieving your goal.

G.R.E.A.T. Goal Activity 8-2

1. Review your goal (or your list of goals if you have several). Are they outcome goals or performance and process goals?
2. If achieving any one of your goals is based on the outcome, take the time now to shift your outcome goals to performance or process goals.
    a. Example: "I will be the top salesperson in my company" can be shifted to "I will attend four networking events per week and send thank you notes to each new contact," which now highlights the individual tasks required to improve your performance to top salesperson status.

In this chapter, you learned about taking 100 percent control and responsibility for your goals to make sure you have Totalitarian control over the outcome. By doing the G.R.E.A.T. Goal Activity above, you now have a written goal (or set of goals) that can be measured by your efforts alone. I hope you are feeling empowered because your goals are now within your ability to achieve!

Congratulations! If you have finished the G.R.E.A.T. Goal Activities so far in this book, you should have at least one clearly defined goal and be poised for success. The next chapter is all about time management and how to map out and systematically plan to achieve your goals.

Nine

Now that you have set a G.R.E.A.T. Goal for yourself, you're well on your way. You have completed the first and (likely) most arduous step, which is figuring out what you want.

Now, how do you get it?

Since you have spent all this time and effort creating your G.R.E.A.T. Goal, I think it is safe to say that now you would like to actually achieve it, right? The difference between a dream and a goal is that a dream is just something you hope will happen. A goal is something you actually decide you want to make happen and then you take focused action. Think of a dream as an idea and a goal as a series of steps designed to turn that idea into reality. Having a plan is the difference between desiring something and actively doing something to achieve that desire. So what do you do first?

Planning Your Journey

You essentially need to create a map to follow. Imagine you are on a journey, and you are trying to get to your desired destination. What is the first thing you need to know to get from here to there? You need to know your starting point. On a map, this is identified with a red 'You Are Here' arrow that points to the spot where you're standing. You can't create a plan or mark a course without knowing your starting and ending points. Your G.R.E.A.T. Goal will be your ending point.

Before any journey begins, you need to prepare for it. You need to know what to pack, how long to plan for, what obstacles you might need to be prepared to work around, what the required investment will be, and the tools and skills you will need to chart your path from start to finish. If you wanted to climb Mount Everest, you would plan ahead and prepare, right? You would research how much it would cost, how long it would take you at a comfortable pace to reach the summit, the best time of year to go, what equipment you might need on your trek, what paperwork you need to have on hand, and who could help you and guide you on the way. You would also probably start physical training well in advance so you'd be fit enough to with-stand the physical hardships. In addition, if you're not retired or still in school, you would need to plan how much time to take off work, and, if you have children, for childcare while you're on your journey. Can you imagine what would happen if you showed up at base camp in shorts and flip flops with no gear and had never walked for more than a mile? Or worse yet, can you imagine if you showed up at the airport to embark on this adventure and didn't have your passport?

Lack of mapping and planning can ruin a journey before it has even begun, and we want to do everything in our power to ensure you reach your final destination.

G.R.E.A.T. Goal Activity 9-1

1. Create a task list of everything that must be accomplished, learned, or mastered to achieve your goal. Don't worry about

having too many steps. It's good to be as detailed as possible. If you don't know everything that is required for every step needed to reach your goal, include research and education as parts of your checklist.

Here's an example of a goal and a corresponding map (task list):

Goal: To give a live workshop six weeks from today on making the most of social networking.

Task list:

- Research topic
- Write presentation
- Create PowerPoint
- Find location for the workshop
- Market the workshop

There are many more tasks and skills needed in order for each individual step to be successful, but you get the idea. You want to be as precise as possible when you make your task list. Let's say that you need to create a PowerPoint presentation, but you don't know how to use PowerPoint. You would then need to add an additional task: either learn PowerPoint or find someone to build the PowerPoint presentation for you.

2. Next to each item on your list, give each skill a letter grade so that you know how proficient you need to be in that category. An A+ means you need to be an expert, a D means you only need minor experience or below average proficiency.
3. Highlight or put a star next to the skills you already have some proficiency in or tasks you have made some progress toward. Give yourself an honest grade for each one. Circle the skills for which you will need to ask for help or learn more about the topic in order to be proficient.

Once your task list is complete, you will have a realistic idea of how far you are from your destination. This is the point in goal setting when many people panic. When they realize just how far they have to go. Stay calm. You want to achieve G.R.E.A.T. things, and that can seem daunting or intimidating. The big picture may seem overwhelming, but like any journey, once you have determined your path, reaching your destination is as simple as putting one foot in front of the other and taking one step at a time.

G.R.E.A.T. Goal Activity 9-2

1. Take three minutes and brainstorm a list of your strengths. They can be physical, mental, skills you have mastered, and so on. Don't be modest, and don't censor yourself.
   Examples: time management, organizational skills, writing, public speaking, computer skills, and so on.
2. Highlight or underline each strength that you can use to help yourself achieve your G.R.E.A.T. Goal.
3. Return to your checklist of skills that must be mastered to reach your goal. For each skill write the corresponding highlighted strength(s) that will help you accomplish this task.
   Example: Task   Strengths to leverage
   Write presentation   Writing, time management, computer skills, organizational skills

It may be tempting to create an excel worksheet and just copy/paste your strengths over and over again. Resist the temptation. Break out a good old-fashioned pad of paper and draw a line down the middle with tasks on the left and strengths to leverage on the right. The tangible act of having your tasks and strengths on physical paper makes the whole process more REAL. You can use your computer to rewrite and reorganize later. For now, make it REAL.

To make your list the most effective tool it can be, under your main steps create a list of subgoals, or single steps (use whichever terminology is preferable to you), needed to accomplish each step. Be crystal clear about every step of this journey so that you are confident and aware of the steps you have accomplished (the progress you have made), and also be certain of the next step you need to take. Confidence and certainty are elements that will be invaluable to you on your goal journey, and the best way to gain and maintain both is to have a clear plan.

G.R.E.A.T. Goal Activity 9-3

1. Take a moment to review your task list from Goal Activity 9-2, including your detailed list of subtasks. Have you forgotten anything? Have you accidently skipped a step or combined two steps in one? Create a master task list of each individual step, double checking to make sure the steps are complete and simple. For example, if one of your steps is to market the workshop, I want you to break it down further.

Task	Steps
Market workshop	Create a website, create a flyer, distribute flyer to local stores, promote on Facebook, place an ad.

   Take a look at the steps above. Are they in the simplest form, or can they be broken down into even smaller steps?

Steps	Simple Steps

| Create a flyer | Write flyer copy, find or create graphics, choose color scheme and font, design layout. |

Don't be surprised if your list seems amazingly long. You are mapping out each individual step, and individual steps are easy to take. Each small step will also be easy to cross off your list once it's complete.

2. What you probably have right now is an overwhelming to-do list. What has to get done first—or what do you want to do first? Logically, you can reorganize by distinguishing what has to be completed in order to tackle the next step. You can't cross the finish line before you cross the starting line; you can't reach the summit before you climb the base of the mountain; you can't run a marathon without finishing the first mile. So determine the best order for your steps. Is it more important to create the flyer first, or is it better to create the website first? Some steps will have a logical progression; others will be your preference of priority. For some steps it will be easier to start with the hardest or least preferable steps, and once each is accomplished, the rest of the journey is easier going. You may prefer to build momentum and gain some progress by starting with some easier steps at the beginning, that way you can attack the harder steps with a little more confidence. Either way is valid. It is just a matter of what works best for you.

3. Now it is time to create a master goal task checklist to work from. There are a variety of ways to accomplish and illustrate this. Choose one of the following styles below—whichever appeals the most to you—or try them all to see which you prefer. If you are more literal and need an exact path to follow, you will likely choose a, b, or c. If you prefer more spontaneity or you like working from a creative, visual outline rather

than a strict list, you will likely choose d or e, as these options let you choose from a set of possible next steps rather than dictating the order.

a. **Master Checklist**. Create a list of your simple step tasks. Rank them in order of importance.

b. **Ladder to Success**. Draw a picture of a ladder. On each rung of the ladder write a task. The lowest rung should be the first task, the highest should be the final task. Go to eyesontheprizebook.com for a printable example.

c. **Goal Map**. Draw a picture of a map complete with the 'You Are Here' arrow and the final destination star. On the path between the two, write each major task in the order you need to take each step. Go to eyesontheprizebook.com for a printable example.

d. **Building Blueprint**. Draw a picture of a pyramid or house. On the lowest layer of the pyramid, or foundation of the house, list all your first steps that need to happen first. On the second layer of the pyramid, or the walls of the house, list the second set of steps that need to be taken. These should not be possible until at least one of the first level steps has been completed. On the third layer of the pyramid, or the roof of the house, list the next set of steps. Finally, on the fourth layer of the pyramid, or the chimney of the house, list the final task. Go to eyesontheprizebook.com for a printable example.

e. **Goal Mind Map**. Create a goal Mind Map (a visual diagram of your interests). Take a sheet of paper and some colored pens or pencils. In the center of the paper, draw a circle (you can use any shape you prefer, but I will refer to circles) and write your overall goal in the center. Now, around the goal circle, draw several smaller circles. Inside each of these circles, write each of your major tasks, using a different color for each task. (This is essentially your task list before you broke it down into simple steps.) With black ink, draw a single line from each major task circle and connect it to the goal circle. Focusing on each major task individually and using the same color as that task, create smaller circles that represent each of your simple steps and branch out toward the edges of the paper. With black ink, draw lines from your simple step circles to the major task circles.

Like I mentioned earlier in this chapter, it is important to have a physical copy of your to-do list. Find a prominent place to display your Mind Map in your workspace, and commit to physically crossing things off as you finish each task.

Once you've completed all the steps in this chapter, you will have a full list of everything you need to do to set and accomplish your goals. Make sure you have posted a physical copy of this goal task list where you will see it on a daily basis, not just jotted down in your notebook, before you move on to the next chapter.

Ten

TAKE YOUR TIME

In the previous chapter, we made a comprehensive task list of everything that needs to be completed in order to achieve your goal. Right now, you most likely have several pages of organized tasks and are feeling a bit overwhelmed. Where do you start? This chapter is about time management, prioritization, and scheduling. By the end of this chapter, you will have cleared your schedule of unnecessary tasks and created a solid timeframe for completing your goal.

The number-one reason my clients give for not completing goals is that they don't have enough time in their already jam-packed days. I counter that not having time is a choice. I'd like you to take a moment to reconsider the phrase "Take your time." Don't think of it as an admonishment to slow down. Think of it as a suggestion to seize, and utilize, your most precious asset—your time. Don't hand it to someone else. Don't spend it on tasks that are unfulfilling. I want you to consciously and consistently make time-use choices that lead you toward your goal. This chapter will give you the tools to control your schedule, prioritize what's important, and take your time.

Time Management

Now that you know what needs to be done, you need to make it a priority. There are many valid and valuable ways of planning out your time. Some prefer to have a daily planner on paper, some prefer a calendar on the wall, some prefer using their phones or Google calendar. You can choose whichever works best for you; there are just two requirements:

1. You must use it consistently.
2. You must look at it every day.

The purpose of scheduling is to make sure you focus on what is most important to you. It does you no good to be sporadic and haphazard with your goal scheduling. It also does you no good to write it down and ignore it.

Many of my clients struggle with an overly full calendar. Their to-do lists are so long that they never reach the end, and tasks just keep rolling over from one day to the next. These lists become overwhelming and exhausting, and as a result, important tasks fall by the wayside. The best way to avoid this pattern is to use three simple steps with everything you put on your calendar: prioritize, delegate, and ignore.

Prioritize

Everything that is a priority should come first. If it is important to you (and everything that helps you reach your goal should be important to you), it should be in your calendar. Only once you have scheduled all your priorities can you then add other tasks. Before you add any task to your schedule, I want you to ask yourself these three questions:

1. Does it help me reach my goal?
2. Do I want to do it?
3. Do *I* need to do it? (Notice this question is not "Does it need to be done?" but rather "Is it necessary that I am the person doing it?")

A task needs to receive at least two yeses to be put on your schedule; otherwise, head to the second step of scheduling—delegate.

Delegate

If it is not a priority but must be done, find someone to pass the task to and hand it off. Some of us think that we need to do everything. We aren't used to asking for (or receiving) help. Part of being productive is recognizing that you don't have to do every task yourself. For example, let's say that you hate vacuuming. It needs to be done, and you don't want to do it. You only have a handful of choices:

- You can make the choice to do the task happily.
- You can dread, postpone, or complain through the entire chore.
- You can ask someone else to do the chore.
- You can pay someone to do the chore.

The beauty of delegation is that someone, somewhere in the world, will be happy or even thrilled to do the task you don't want to do. Everyone has different skill sets. Everyone has different passions. There's no shame in calling in the reserves to help get the job done.

This rule doesn't just have to apply to things you don't *want* to do. It can also apply to things that aren't worth your time or energy to do. For example, if building a website is on your to-do list and you don't have the skill set to do it (or you have the skill set, but it will take you three times as long as a web designer to get it done), hire someone. You don't have to be a one-person band. If a task needs to be done, and you don't personally need to do it, make the most of your time and productivity and pass this job on to someone else.

Ignore

If a task does not get a single *yes* to the above questions, don't put it on your schedule. Give yourself permission to ignore it. Guilt free. Your time and focus are too important to waste on this task.

In an ideal, high-performance calendar, 70 percent of your schedule should be tasks that have garnered three yeses, and 30 percent should garner two yeses. This can be a difficult transition for some of you. It's hard to ignore some tasks and let go of the guilt. For now, you will work on creating a more balanced and maintainable schedule with the following breakdown: 50 percent of your total scheduled time will be filled with three-yes tasks, 35 percent with two-yes tasks, and 15 percent with one-yes tasks.

G.R.E.A.T. Goal Activity 10-1

1. We are going to make room in your existing calendar for new activities.
   a. Look at your current schedule and answer the following three questions for each task currently on your calendar:
      1. Does it help me reach my goal?
      2. Do I want to do it?
      3. Do *I* need to do it?
   b. Remove all items that only receive one yes, and save that list.

2. Review your master goal task checklist from the previous chapter (Goal Activity 9-3) and answer the three questions for each task. Analyze what percentage of your time is currently dedicated to three-yes tasks, two-yes tasks, and one-yes tasks. Add the two- and three-yes tasks to the list to be added to your schedule. (We will actually put these tasks in your schedule shortly.) How close are you to the balanced schedule described above?

3. Make a list of all your tasks that have only received one yes Choose which tasks you will delegate and which you will ignore. (Note: If it is from your master goal task checklist in chapter 9, it can't be ignored). For those you choose to delegate, assign a person to whom you will delegate.

4. Create a list that contains all the leftover one-yes tasks that you have chosen to ignore. You have determined that these are not a valuable or important way to spend your time. Rip that list into tiny little pieces and throw it away. Doesn't that feel good?

Scheduling Tactics

There are numerous theories and tactics available to help you schedule your time. To cover all of them would fill an entire second book. So I will simply say that you should choose the method of scheduling that works best for you, but you must consistently keep track. It doesn't matter if you use an online calendar or go old school and write it in a notebook. The organization and accountability an actual schedule will provide is necessary to reach complicated goals. Make sure you devote enough time so that you can actually reach your goal. Be sure you block that time in your calendar and make it a priority.

If you know you work better in the morning, schedule your time then. Statistically, you are more likely to accomplish a task that is scheduled in the morning because emergencies are less likely to get in the way. Additionally, willpower reserves are stronger, making it more likely that you will stick to and follow through with your plan. Or if you are a night owl and can barely function in the morning, by all means schedule in the evening. If you focus really well in short bursts, schedule accordingly. However, if starting is the hard part but once you get going you can continue on for hours, it may be better to schedule fewer but longer blocks of goal time.

Next, I want you to break your goal tasks into monthly lists. You might think, "Hold up! *Monthly* lists?" We have talked quite a bit about breaking larger tasks into smaller, more manageable bites, so you probably think day-by-day planning would be most effective at reaching your long-term goal. This is not always the case.

Studies have shown that monthly planning, or even weekly planning, leads to bigger improvements over longer periods of time. The drawback of intense daily planning is that the preparation can be incredibly time consuming. It can take much longer to make thirty individual daily plans than it takes to create one broader, monthly plan. The daily plan also lacks flexibility, so it can feel like you're forced into a series of steps with little choice in the matter. Not to mention, life is unpredictable, and once you have one off day on a daily plan, you can get frustrated. One off day can affect your motivation and morale, and you are more likely to assume failure and stop altogether. The monthly plan allows you the ability to change and adjust as needed to reach your goal. If life throws you for a loop one day, you can always pick back up the next day and still reach your goal.

I recommend that you consistently block out the time and create a weekly, bi-weekly, or monthly task list from which you can choose your tasks. Schedule major goal landmarks to keep on track.

The easiest way to schedule your goal steps is to work backward. When do you want to have this goal completed? For simplicity's sake, we will make our example six months away. Go to that day in your calendar and type (or write) "Congratulations! Goal reached!" Then write what your goal was. Now go to the middle point of the calendar (for this example, three months away) and on that day type (or write) "Halfway there! On the homestretch!" Now list what you need to have accomplished on your journey at this point to be halfway finished. Continue to break it down, writing on your calendar what needs to be done at the quarter mark and at the three-quarter mark.

Repeat this process until you have broken down your goal tasks into month-long or two-week long chunks.

G.R.E.A.T. Goal Activity 10-2

1. Block out your time on your calendar for your goal-oriented tasks as I have described in Goal Activity 9-2. Make sure to keep this blocked-out time a priority. Remember to take into account your most productive times of the day and your preferred length of time blocks.

2. Divide the goal task list you created in chapter 9 into monthly blocks. Write those tasks on a page and put it in your calendar. Use an existing calendar and designate it as your goal calendar, or write each month on a large sheet of paper, or draw the current month on a dry erase board and hang it on the wall of your primary workspace. Hang only the current month you are working on, and be sure to cross out, check mark, or star each task you have completed. If you are using an online calendar, assign a specific color or symbol to your goal tasks so they visually stand out from the rest of your

schedule. Actively cross out the tasks (or change the color or symbol) as you complete them.

3. Add all the additional three- and two-yes tasks that do not pertain to your goal back in your schedule, if there is room.

Taking control of your scheduling and managing your time well is essential to reaching your G.R.E.A.T. Goal. Spending time on what is important to you, putting your goals and priorities first, and learning to remove what is unnecessary is not only productive but empowering. Be consistent with your schedule. It may seem difficult at first, but remember, you get really good at what you practice. You just need to practice habits that help you achieve.

As you stick to your goal and check off items on your list, you may find that your overall happiness and satisfaction with your life increases. You've made time for what is important and are taking steps toward achieving it. You have stopped wasting time beating yourself up about things that aren't important and are only spending time on things that are meaningful to you. If that isn't the definition of a self-motivated, purpose-driven life, I don't know what is!

Eleven

Sometimes the hardest part of going for your goals is crossing the no-man's-land that exists between change and transition. Simply put, change is temporary. Change is deciding that you are going to accomplish your goals. Transition is what must happen to make a change permanent—to achieve your goals. Transition is a process, and it must be completed lest you go back to how you were before you decided to make a change. This chapter will focus on the stages of transition and why it's important to complete the process.

Transition

Transition is a psychological three-stage process that people go through as they accept and come to terms with the new situation that change brings. If you want change to work, to stick, to become a way of life, or to become a permanent habit, you must go through a transition. Getting through this transition is essential if the change is actually to work as planned.

The End

Transitions begin with an end. It is paradoxical but true. Think of a big change that may have happened in your life: having a baby, getting a promotion to a new department, moving to another city. Each one of these transitions starts with letting go. With a baby, you may have to let go of sleep, spontaneity, time with your spouse, alone time. With a promotion to a new department, you may lose your coworkers and peers, and maybe you also lose that feeling of expertise that comes with doing work with which you were familiar. With a physical move, you lose the sense of familiarity you once had. You leave behind all the connections in your neighborhood like the dry cleaner, your favorite coffee shop, and the next-door neighbor who babysat for you. Even though these are most likely all good changes, there is still a sense of loss associated with them.

G.R.E.A.T Goal Activity 11-1

1. Make a list of everything that you will lose or that will change in the process of reaching toward and achieving your goal. Even if it seems like something you want to lose, add it to the list.
    Example Goal: I will write a screenplay in the next six months.
    Possible Losses:
    *   I will have to miss out on important family, friend, and work functions.
    *   I will have to lose spontaneity in my schedule and become more structured.
    *   I will have to be vulnerable and expose myself to criticism and uncomfortable feedback.
    *   I will have to give up on the potential dream (of writing a blockbuster and my life becomes amazing overnight) and focus on the reality, which might not live up to my expectations.

Sense of Identity

Our image and identity, who we think we are, are largely defined by our roles and relationships, those we like as well as those we don't. We come to identify with the circumstances of our lives. We assign ourselves titles for our relationships like mom, dad, brother, sister, friend, or coworker. We also embrace our work personas with yet other titles like entrepreneur, teacher, systems analyst, or breadwinner. Imagine meeting someone new. You stick out your hand to introduce yourself: "Hi, I'm So and So. I'm a _____." That blank is usually your relationship to something in the situation: elementary school teacher, soccer mom, CFO of a virtual-reality startup, and so on.

Changing means changing our perception of ourselves. By going after your goal, if it's big enough, the familiarity and relationships you have will likely change as a result. Your titles, your circle of coworkers and friends, the things you do every day will either change completely or will go through a period of adjustment.

By their very nature, these kinds of transitions are uncomfortable. It is why people resist change. The journey of transition—departing from the known and familiar and steering toward the risk of the unknown and unfamiliar—is not easy. But acknowledging there is more comfort in going backward than going forward will help you resist turning around. If you were really happy there, why are you trying to change now?

G.R.E.A.T. Goal Activity 11-2

1. Take a few minutes to write about the feelings you have when you consider attempting and achieving your goal. Pay specific attention to any negative emotions or doubts.
2. Now take a few moments and write about your feelings when you consider never attempting or achieving your goal.

3. Brainstorm all the titles, traits, and qualities you have that make up your image and identity. List the good and the bad.

Attitude

So how do we deal with the ending that comes as a result of your transition? To successfully navigate these changes, you will need to understand your attitude toward change. Our attitudes and coping mechanisms start early. Think back to your childhood, your formative years, and identify three transitions you went through. Some may be large and terrible, a death in the family, for instance. Others may have been insignificant to everyone except you: the loss of a pet, changing schools, losing trust in someone, or losing faith in something. It could simply be a family vacation, moving to a new home, or even a new haircut.

Now think back to those transitions and try to remember your response to when things ended. The inner element in that response is a mental state or frame of mind. The mood can be difficult to identify, but by looking back on old endings, you are likely to realize that your mindset is being reactivated in the present. How you reacted to change in your formative years can give a clue to how you react on a gut level as an adult.

Often the emotions you feel as an adult are triggered by events you experienced in your formative years. If you moved as a child and it was filled with stress and drama, it is possible that those memories and anxiety are triggered when faced with a move as an adult.

When you look back over your past endings, what can you say about your own style of bringing situations to a close? Is it abrupt and designed to deny the impact of the change? Or is it so slow and gradual it is hard to see that anything important is happening? Is it your initiative that brings things to term or do events just happen to you? See if you can identify your transition style within the family context. Are you the calm, steady one? Maybe you are the dramatic center of attention?

If you can't recognize your own ending style, don't fret. While it's advantageous to understand your style of ending, some part of you will resist that understanding as though your life depended on it. If you can't answer your ending-style questions, instead think about how you tend to end a night out or an evening at a friend's house. Do you try to drag things out by starting new conversations and activities when others are moving toward the door? Or do you suddenly say good-night and dash out? There are no wrong answers—you are just getting to know yourself.

G.R.E.A.T. Goal Activity 11-3

1. List three transitions from your childhood or formative years. How did they end?
2. Take a moment to write down three words that describe your personal ending style.

The Neutral Zone

In the space between an ending and a beginning is a time filled with emptiness, a feeling of being lost, and sometimes chaos. It's the Neutral Zone. In modern times, we have trouble with the Neutral Zone because, for many of us, emptiness represents only the absence of something, and what is missing is the important part.

Picture a wide river. The water is rushing past at a good pace. On the other bank is something you want, so you decide to hop in and swim to the other side (or in a different scenario, maybe someone pushes you in and you have no choice but to swim). The Ending is when you leave the bank of the river. You are saying good-bye to the solid security of the land and all that is familiar and safe. You paddle to the middle of the river, you are alone, and you are getting tired. You are worried about your chances and wonder if you have made the right choice; maybe leaving the bank was a bad idea. You are not sure you have the strength to get to the other side, where it is, or why it was important to get there in the first place. You may even regret the choice to swim away from what, in hindsight, looks like a good thing. At this point, most people do one of two things: They either turn around and head back to where they started from, or they take a deep breath and paddle as fast as possible to the other side.

In case you haven't figured it out, the middle of the river is the Neutral Zone. An in-between time where you are past the majority of the grieving and it seems like nothing much is happening, but you are doing the important inner business of self-transformation. When you're in the Neutral Zone, you begin to understand the world differently. This is also the time where you naturally reenergize so you can face the next step, which is the new Beginning.

For many people, the Neutral Zone is characterized by physical and mental stress. Some hunker down and suffer through this zone. Others learn to adapt by recognizing these Neutral Zone moments and actually carving a time-out period for themselves.

People who can recognize when they are in a Neutral Zone and give themselves down time often have a healthier attitude toward change and approach transition with less anxiety. They also come back reinvigorated, reenergized, and ready to face the next phase: the new Beginning.

G.R.E.A.T. Goal Activity 11-4

1. Find a way to celebrate releasing your losses. It can be as simple as burning or shredding the piece of paper you have

written them down on or as elaborate as holding a wake in their honor. It can be public or private, but it is a way of wrapping up the grieving process and embarking on the journey to the next zone.

2. Take a moment to see if you can identify your default reaction to the Neutral Zone. Do you wallow? Do you rush? Do you try to skip it altogether? List five examples of how you handled (or didn't handle) the Neutral Zone in the past.

3. What is the scariest thing about the Neutral Zone for you? What is the most exciting?

Five Suggestions to Getting Unstuck in the Neutral Zone—Stay Steady

If you feel like you are getting stuck, don't worry. There are five powerful steps you can take to free yourself.

1. **Surrender**. Don't fight the process. If you fight the Neutral Zone, you may wind up stuck and wallowing and decide it's easier to go back to the way things were before.

2. **Take Your Time**. Accept the need for time. You can't rush the Neutral Zone. If you skip or speed up the Neutral Zone, you won't be focused and energized enough to start the new Beginning, and you will go back to where you started. You may even be forced to repeat the entire process.

3. **Keep a Journal**. Begin a log of experiences. Keep it simple: record moods and record exactly what was happening, not just a daily log of events. Later, you may not remember much that happened in the Neutral Zone. Your time in the Neutral Zone might seem like a blur. Rereading this journal can help remind you what you learned during the process.

4. **Embrace Being Alone.** Find a regular time and place to be alone. This will give you undistracted thinking time. You may feel like you're not doing anything productive. It may seem like you are just gardening, or taking a walk, or sitting, but you are clearing the distractions and noise and giving yourself time to process your new experiences.

5. **Discover What You Really Want.** Knowing what you want is far less clear than it would seem. Our wants are often tangled up with a lifetime of guilt and ambivalence. This is your chance to make sure your new Beginning is what you want, not something you are settling for, or what someone else wants for you, or something you think you should want.

G.R.E.A.T. Goal Activity 11-5

1. Pretend you just learned you won't live to see the sun rise tomorrow. What three things would you consider your greatest achievements? What three things do you wish you had done?

2. Take a few minutes or a few days to go on your own version of a rite of passage. Hike up a mountain and back, build a fire and stay up all night watching it, take some down time and create a piece of art. Give yourself the chance to fully experience the Neutral Zone. Embrace it, and make the most of it.

The Beginning

Once you complete the Ending and the Neutral Zone, you are off to the Beginning, which is where most people try to start. The Beginning is where you implement the new change into your life, and you move forward to achieve your goals. If you are able to successfully complete the Ending and the Neutral Zone, the first two stages of transition, it is more likely that the changes you are making will stick.

G.R.E.A.T. Goal Activity 11-6

1. List five times you set a goal or tried to make a transition that was not successful. For each attempt, identify which stage of transition you got stuck in or where you quit.
2. With your new understanding about the process of transition, what could you have done differently in each of these five unsuccessful attempts?
3. With your new goal, what will you do differently this time to make this a transition and not just a change? Were there any steps in the transition process that you struggled with or hurried through or even abandoned altogether? What decisions can you make or actions can you take to make this transition successful?

Transitions make the world go round, and without an ending you can't have a beginning. Understanding more about the process of transitions, the three stages of a transition, Endings, the Neutral Zone, and Beginnings, gives you a better idea of what to expect and how to get through all of them. You are attempting to achieve your G.R.E.A.T. Goals, and to do that, you must make changes in your life. Transitions aren't scary, they are necessary, if you want the change to last.

Twelve

Mindset

In the last chapter, we learned about change versus transition. Transition is the mental process that makes change permanent. This chapter will arm you with one of the primary tools you will need to push through the challenges of transition. Read on for more about mindset and how the attitude you bring to your journey can influence whether or not you achieve your goal.

What is the difference between an obstacle and an excuse? Some people believe the former is a challenge you can conquer, while the latter is a justification for failure, one you can't overcome. For most people, the difference between an obstacle and an excuse is a question of control: Is the problem something you can work to get past, or is it something out of your control that will force you to stop your journey?

Growth versus Fixed

Mindset is the attitude and perspective with which you approach change and challenges. Mindset is often visualized as a spectrum with opposing ideals at each end: *growth* and *fixed*. Most people fall somewhere between the two. I prefer to imagine it like a teeter-totter. Depending on the timing or the situation, you might be closer to a *fixed mindset* (the ground) or you might be closer to a *growth mindset* (soaring in the air). The goal of the teeter-totter is to use the ground to push off so you can rise back up, instead of staying solidly stuck to the earth or staying in the air the entire time.

People in a growth mindset believe that their true potential is unknown and that it's impossible to truly predict what they can accomplish. With effort, there is no limit to what people can achieve. They believe that basic qualities and skills are things that can be cultivated through effort. They have a passion for stretching themselves, and they aren't daunted by hard work. In fact, they are very good at sticking to a task despite obstacles. They thrive on learning, are excited by challenges, and embrace expanding their comfort zones. They choose to surround themselves with people who challenge and excite them.

People in a fixed mindset believe that their qualities are innate and fixed in stone. This belief sometimes creates an urgency to continuously prove themselves. They hide or cover up deficiencies instead of attempting to overcome them. They like activities that they are immediately good at because they enjoy activities that reinforce their strengths. They believe that success is the goal and have a hard time believing that any good comes from failure. They thrive in their comfort zone, and they like to stay safely within it. They look for friends and partners that will shore up their self-esteem rather than challenge them.

Both mindsets are great at setting goals, and surprisingly both are great at reaching goals. The difference comes in when we evaluate the scope of the goals and the energy and enthusiasm with which each mindset tackles their goals. Growth mindset tends to focus on the process and strategy goals: the steps within their control that will help them achieve their goals. Fixed mindset tends to focus on the end result over the process. Both can be high achievers, but the difference is in how they approach tasks that are beyond their current scope of success.

A perfect example of the differences is a study that was shared in the book *Mindset: The New Psychology of Success* by Carol S. Dweck. In one example, fifth graders were each given a simple puzzle to do, which they all enjoyed. Then the children were given a much more challenging puzzle to complete. Surprisingly, those with a fixed mindset showed a massive depreciation in enjoyment, even if they were able to finish the puzzle. Some even fibbed so they wouldn't have to take the puzzles home to practice. The children with a growth mindset were most excited by the hard problems and wanted to take them home to practice more.

Those with the growth mindset embraced the challenge of learning even if it involved failing, while those with the fixed mindset focused on the achievement of the goal and the ease with which it was obtained.

Which is your default mindset? Growth or fixed? Remember I mentioned that we are all a bit of both, so ask yourself, which mindset do you exhibit when you are at your best? Which do you show when you are in a time of crisis or challenge? Which do you need in order to achieve the challenge you have set for yourself?

Shift That Mindset

I believe the only difference between an obstacle and an excuse is your mindset. Do you choose to see it as a challenge you can surpass or get around (obstacle), or do you let it stop you and use it as a justification for your lack of success (excuse)? The G.R.E.A.T. Goal achiever is a master at turning excuses into obstacles. Mindset is about recognizing the power of your outlook. You can choose to let something stop you, or you can decide to take the action you need to overcome it. Instead of looking at a challenge as insurmountable, figure out a way to make it possible. Reframing an excuse into an obstacle can be as easy as asking one question: What can I do to get to the other side?

Picture your excuse as a solid twenty-foot-high brick wall right in front of you, stretching in both directions as far as you can see. Your goal is just on the other side waiting for you. It seems impossible and unreachable, and it is, if you decide to accept the wall as an excuse. But what if you ask yourself, "What can I do to get to the other side?" Here are some answers my clients came up with:

- "I would get a sledge hammer and make a door."
- "I would scale the wall like a rock climber and get over the top."
- "I would call ten friends and have them make a human pyramid to lift me to the top."
- And my personal favorite: "I would build a catapult and throw myself over."

The greatest enemy to any excuse is your mind—your determination, your outlook, and your creativity. If you choose to let something stop you, it will; but if you choose to reframe it, you can make it a mere obstacle that you can overcome.

Don't panic if you have realized that your mindset is more fixed than you would like it to be. The good news is you can shift your mindset with consistent practice. Here are a few tips to help you:

1. Focus on strategy or process goals rather than outcome goals.
2. Praise your effort rather than your mastery.
3. Actively challenge yourself to attempt new things that are outside of your comfort zone. Try them a second time, even if you sucked the first time.

4. Identify situations that you have previously approached with a fixed mindset, and take time before the situation or task to remind yourself of the value of a growth mindset.

G.R.E.A.T. Goal Activity 12-1

1. Brainstorm a list of all the reasons you have not yet accomplished your G.R.E.A.T. Goal.
2. Create a list of all the things that may stop you or slow you down while you are on the path to achieving your goal.
3. Look at both lists. Which are obstacles and which are excuses?
4. How can you reframe the excuses so they become obstacles?
5. What skills, strengths, or opportunities can you leverage to overcome these obstacles?

Putting an End to Excuses

Below is a list of common excuses and an example of how you can reframe each excuse into a challenge you can overcome:

- Not enough time: How can I make time in my schedule to reach my goal?
- Not enough money: How can I shift my income to reach this goal or shift the expenses to make my goal reachable?
- Don't have the knowledge: Where or how can I get the knowledge I need to reach my goal?
- Don't have the connections: How do I create the network I need to reach my goal?

Now that you know how to use your mindset to turn excuses into obstacles and effectively get around them, we'll move on to another key to transition in the next chapter—finding motivation and keeping your momentum. Keep reading. Momentum is currently on your side!

Thirteen

MOTIVATION

I n the last chapter, you learned how important mindset is when approaching your goals. This chapter will arm you with the tools you will need to push through the hard times and just keep going—so you can achieve your goals. Read on for more about motivation and the power of momentum in your journey to achieve your goal.

Motivation

When Isaac Newton came up with the first law of motion—an object at rest tends to stay at rest, and an object in motion tends to stay in motion—he was referring to the laws of physics and movement, but this rule also applies to goal achievement. This law, which is also called the law of inertia, states that it is harder to start a movement than it is to continue a movement. It takes more energy to begin than it does to continue. This means that it's much more difficult to start and stop multiple times than it is to continue on at a steady pace. In fact, each time you stop, you waste time, energy, momentum, and it is less likely that you will start up again.

Being consistently motivated, and taking diligent action with that motivation, is the key to transforming your goal to your reality. It doesn't matter if it takes a month, a year, or ten years. As long as you can continue to make progress and move forward, you will reach your goal. It is when you stop that success is doomed. I guess this chapter is as much about consistency as it is about motivation, but I find the two go hand in hand.

Remember Aesop's fable about the tortoise and the hare? They ran a race, and the hare would sprint ahead, then laze about and rest, then sprint ahead, then laze about some more. All the while the tortoise plodded on at a slow and steady pace. We all know what happened. The tortoise won the contest, and the moral of this fable is "slow and steady wins the race." I think the moral of this tale is that consistent action and motivation lead to success. The slow part is not important but being steady is. When faced with a seemingly impossible goal, the tortoise does not stop. He does not make excuses. He does not justify his certain loss or lament the unfairness of the match. He simply moves, steadily, one step at a time, toward the finish line. Focused, consistent, and motivated. And he wins. He wins because an object in motion tends to stay in motion.

I should tell my clients to be a tortoise, but I don't—who wants to think of themselves as a slow, ponderous creature? Instead, I tell my clients to picture themselves as the "rolling stone" in the old proverb that "gathers no moss." Be a ROCK: firm, steady, and a force to be reckoned with when in motion.

Reminders

Have you have heard the saying "out of sight, out of mind"? Your goal should always be on the forefront of your mind. To make it a priority, you have to think about it. Earlier in this book I asked you to remind yourself of your goal every day, because daily reminders not only increase consistency but they help to continually emphasize that you have chosen to make this goal a priority. These next activities will help you come up with many creative ways to remind yourself of the G.R.E.A.T. Goal you are working toward and to encourage you on your path.

G.R.E.A.T. Goal Activity 13-1

1. Write your goal on a full sheet of paper (or print it out in bold). Hang it where it will be the first thing you see when you open your eyes in the morning and the last thing you see when you close your eyes at night.
2. Write words of encouragement on sticky notes and place them throughout your house, car, and office.
3. Create a short, specific mantra that motivates you and post it in a place you see on a daily basis like your office wall, fridge door, or phone screensaver.
4. Create five motivational anchors for yourself. An anchor is an object that you see on a daily basis that can relate in some way to your goal or what you are trying to achieve. For example, one of my clients who was working on increasing her level of fitness chose the following anchors:
    *   A picture of a tree in her living room. Trees are strong, have deep roots, yet continue to reach for the sky and grow like she is doing.
    *   A wedding ring. This is a change she wants to make so she can live a long healthy life with her husband.
    *   Tennis shoes. Movement is fun, and the closer she gets to her goal, the easier it will become.

- A hummingbird feeder outside her window. Hummingbirds are the ultimate metabolizers. They only eat what they need to survive, and they burn what they eat so efficiently they must eat five to ten times an hour.
- Her fridge. When to open the door and eat is her conscious choice, and so she has control over her food decisions.

Once you have chosen your five anchors, remind yourself of their meanings each time you see one.

5. Start a goal journal. Each night write everything you have done that day to bring you closer to your goal.

Sharing

Now it's time to share your goal with others. Sharing your goal makes you more accountable. It also allows others to encourage you or help you along the way. Many of us shy away from sharing our goals for fear of being judged or discouraged. I say be proud of your goal and share it. There is great motivation in the commitment of sharing a goal with the world.

There are two things that happen psychologically when you share a goal. First, it makes your commitment to your goal concrete in a way that all your reading and planning can't do. By saying it out loud, your goal is no longer living in your head. It is out in the world free to grow and be fulfilled. All kidding aside, owning your goals and saying what you want, why you want it, and how you are going to get it, out loud, to an audience, makes your commitment real in a way that spreadsheets and notebooks never can.

Second, by telling friends and family your goals, you are giving yourself an audience. Nobody wants to fail in front of an audience, and success is always sweeter when you receive recognition for it. A little applause never hurt anybody. No one wants to bump into a friend a year later and have them say, "Hey! What happened to that plan of yours…" and you have to confess that you haven't made any progress. You won't let that happen. You won't invite people to watch you fail. You are gathering an audience to cheer you as you succeed.

Beware! Not everyone will be excited and enthusiastic about your goals. There are people in this world who like the status quo and resist change, even good change, because it makes them uncomfortable. You can recognize these people by their questions, their skeptical expressions, their sarcasm. When faced with a negative reaction to your goals, keep in mind that their reaction is not about you; it is about them and their fear. Choose to find more supportive people to share with in the future and move on.

Accountability

Take sharing one step further and find an accountability partner to check in with on a regular basis. Studies have shown that people with an accountability partner greatly increase their odds of reaching their goal and tend to achieve their goal faster. Your partner is not there to give you motivation or keep you on track. He or she shouldn't shame or chastise you if you didn't complete a step or reward you if you exceed your expectations. Your partner is merely an additional way of tracking progress and maintaining motivation. An effective accountability partner should really ask only three questions:

1. Did you accomplish the steps you set for yourself since the last check-in?
2. If not, what did you choose to do instead?
3. What will you have accomplished by our next check-in?

Your accountability person should be someone you trust and can count on but also someone who is not personally invested in the outcome of your goal. If you choose a partner who stands to gain something personally from your achievement, it may be difficult for him or her to keep your best interests at heart. The best accountability partners are people who are trying to achieve something similar and want you to hold them accountable as well. Just be sure that your motivation is independent of each other. If your partner doesn't make a step, it does not make it okay for you not to make a step.

Willpower

When you combine focus and self-control to take consistent action toward your goal, you are tapping into your willpower. When the path gets difficult and you want to turn back, it is willpower that keeps you moving forward. In the past, willpower was conceptually viewed as a bank account that filled itself back up overnight. You had a finite amount of willpower to get you through the day, so it was best to conserve it and dole it out wisely so that you always had some in reserve if an extreme need came up.

Now we know that willpower is more like muscle. The more you practice and work it out, the stronger and more resilient it becomes. Like weight training a muscle, you can work out your willpower to the point of fatigue, which is the point when you make a choice that may take you off track. But the next time you practice willpower, you can push further before you hit the wall. Also like working out your muscles, it is consistent training and practice that leads to the best results. If you don't go to the gym for a month, what happens on the first day you're back? You are not as strong, and your endurance has weakened. Athletes train their muscles; G.R.E.A.T. Goal setters train their willpower.

G.R.E.A.T. Goal Activity 13-2

1. Make a list of at least three people to share your goal with. Then share it.
2. If you are on a social network, and you are comfortable sharing in this format, share your goal in a post or blog.
3. Create a list of possible accountability partners. Choose one, and ask if he or she is willing to check-in with you once a week.
4. What is one way you can practice consistent willpower? It is best to start with something easy and gradually increase the difficulty.

Track

Keep track of your progress, so you know how far you have come and how much farther you have to go. This can be as simple as hanging a copy of your step-by-step list on the wall and crossing things off as you go, to creating an excel spreadsheet to track your progress. You could go old school with a gold star chart and give yourself a star every time you accomplish a task!

Tracking also allows you to set milestones to gauge your progress. Be sure to celebrate each milestone in some way that inspires or excites you. It can be a happy dance, or a special meal, a day of adventure, or even a physical reward, if you prefer. I had one client who created a reward grab bag. Every time she saw something she wanted but didn't need, she would buy it and immediately put it in her reward grab bag. For every milestone she hit, she allowed herself to choose one thing from the bag. Physical rewards do not have to be expensive to be effective. Each reward in her bag was under ten dollars.

If you choose to physically reward yourself for your milestones, remember to focus on the joy of accomplishing the milestone as much as you focus on the reward—we don't want you to become solely focused on prizes. Also, if you choose to reward yourself, you must absolutely give yourself the reward you have earned. No postponing until the next milestone or telling yourself you don't really need it since you have already leveraged the motivation to get where you are. If you don't follow through with your reward, it will no longer be an effective motivation tool. If you tell your children you will take them out for ice cream if they clean their room, but once the room is cleaned you change your mind, the next time you offer a reward for a clean room, they will know you are being untruthful. The same thing holds true for you. If you don't follow through with your promise to yourself, it becomes a lie.

G.R.E.A.T. Goal Activity 13-3

1. Create your own tracking system and put it into action.
2. Determine what your measurable milestones will be and what your celebrations and rewards will be as well.

Basic Needs

This one is common sense, but it is so important it bears repeating. Self-care is essential to help you reach your goal. Have you heard of Maslow's hierarchy of needs? It is a simple pyramid that breaks down our fundamental needs based on importance. Maslow discovered that certain basic (physiological) needs must be fulfilled before we can focus on growth (self-actualization) needs. What does that mean for the G.R.E.A.T. Goal setter? You must take care of the basics first. You need proper nutrition, proper sleep, proper shelter, and proper safety in place before you can focus on your goals. And you must maintain these needs to continue your growth. Your goal should be built on a strong foundation of self-care. Skimping on basic needs will slow your momentum and may even make it impossible for you to reach your goal. I have seen many a goal setter sacrifice basic needs to reach their goal thinking they are being incredibly committed and focused. But what they are really doing is sabotaging themselves. If you're not eating right, getting enough sleep, or exercising, how can you possibly succeed at a challenge? One of the keys to achieving a G.R.E.A.T. Goal is to take great care of yourself.

Get eight hours of sleep a night. Eighty percent of us need eight hours of sleep a night, 10 percent function best on less, and 10 percent on more. If you don't get enough sleep, your cognitive skills slow, your decision-making skills become impaired, your motivation decreases, and your stress levels increase.

Eat three healthy meals a day. Proper nutrition provides fuel for you to work smoothly and efficiently all day. Blood sugar drops or spikes can decrease productivity, reduce focus and attention span, and increase irritability. Lack of proper vitamins and minerals can affect brain function and learning ability.

Move that body. Walk, run, skip, lift weights, ride a bike. Move for thirty minutes a day. Being out of shape is not only bad for your health it's inefficient for goal achievement. It decreases productivity, endurance, and stamina—all things you need to reach your goal.

Execute

Once you start moving, don't stop. Do something every day that will bring you closer to your goal. Remember, it is harder to start again if you stop, so keep the momentum going and keep moving forward.

There is a quote my dad used to tell me all the time growing up: "How do you eat an elephant? One bite at a time."

How do you reach your G.R.E.A.T. Goal? One step at a time. So take a step. Just one. Then repeat.

Are you ready to go out there and get started? After reading this chapter, I hope you realize that once you get started, it is much easier to keep going, keep pushing, keep checking off things on your list every day. Don't stop. Don't lose your momentum. It is harder to restart than to just keep going. Tell a friend, get an accountability partner, and keep moving forward.

Fourteen

CONCLUSION

Congratulations! If you have completed all the steps and activities in this book, you are well on your way to success. You have a Genuine, Reachable, Exact, Affirmative, and Totalitarian goal. You have spelled out why you want your goal and exactly how to achieve it. You have prioritized your duties and created action plans for tackling them. You have carved out time in your schedule to dedicate to the completion of each step, delegated your lesser responsibilities to others, and thrown away responsibilities that don't move you forward. You have mentally prepared yourself not only to enact change but to transition to new, permanent habits. If it seems like a lot—you're right. You have already accomplished more than most people ever will and are prepared to attain the G.R.E.A.T. Goal you have set your mind to achieve.

Do you feel empowered? Do you feel that knot of strength that comes from knowing exactly what you need to do and knowing exactly how to go about doing it? Do you feel excited? Not just for today but for tomorrow and every step of your journey as well?

There are a number of resources available to help you on your journey. In addition to my workshop and coaching services available at rainshadowcoaching.com, the last section of this book contains a list of related books. Some of them were source and research material for this book. Some are classic business and success books. All are good reading to help keep you focused and in tune with your goal. I would encourage you to read from this list in your downtime and not as a replacement for goal-achieving activities. The time for doing is now. No excuses.

Below is a poem I would like to share with you. As you embark on your G.R.E.A.T. Goal, there may be days that are more productive than others. There will be times you are overwhelmed or discouraged. I find this poem to be a great reminder that we can't control or change the past; we can only control the choices we make today and choose the future we want to create.

"Start Where You Stand" by Berton Braley
Start where you stand and never mind the past,
The past won't help you in beginning new,
If you have left it all behind at last
Why, that's enough, you're done with it, you're through;
This is another chapter in the book,
This is another race that you have planned,
Don't give the vanished days a backward look,
Start where you stand.

The world won't care about your old defeats
If you can start anew and win success;
The future is your time, and time is fleet
And there is much of work and strain and stress;
Forget the buried woes and dead despairs,

Here is a brand-new trial right at hand,
The future is for him who does and dares,
Start where you stand.

Old failures will not halt, old triumphs aid,
To-day's the thing, to-morrow soon will be;
Get in the fight and face it unafraid,
And leave the past to ancient history,
What has been, has been; yesterday is dead
And by it you are neither blessed nor banned;
Take courage, man, be brave and drive ahead,
Start where you stand.

"Start Where You Stand" is a fantastic reminder. Leave the past in the past. Leave the future for tomorrow. The choices that you make today are those that matter. Concentrate on today, this moment, to drive forward and achieve your goals.

I want to leave you with a last little bit of inspiration. The following is a poem by William Ernest Henley. I pull this out on days when I feel overwhelmed and need a reminder about empowerment and perseverance. It has inspired countless leaders, entrepreneurs, and artists since it was first published in 1888.

"Invictus" by William Ernest Henley
Out of the night that covers me,
Black as the pit from pole to pole,
I thank whatever gods may be
For my unconquerable soul.

In the fell clutch of circumstance
I have not winced nor cried aloud.

Under the bludgeonings of chance
My head is bloody, but unbowed.

Beyond this place of wrath and tears
Looms but the horror of the shade,
And yet the menace of the years
Finds, and shall find, me unafraid.

It matters not how strait the gate,
How charged with punishments the scroll,
I am the master of my fate:
I am the captain of my soul.

Think about those last two lines: "I am the master of my fate. I am the captain of my soul." Does this resonate with you? You have a goal that is 100 percent within your control and a plan for how to achieve it. You have picked your crew. You have picked your course. You are most assuredly the master of your fate and the captain of your soul.

In chapter 1 of this book, I said there is nothing more fulfilling to me than helping clients discover and then achieve their goals. I want to take this opportunity to ask you to share your story with me. I would be honored to hear about your journey toward your goal: your struggles and your triumphs. Please e-mail me at goals@rainshadow-coaching.com. Your success means more to me than you can possibly imagine.

I wish you all the best in your endeavors. Go out and get your G.R.E.A.T. Goal. Then set the next and keep going. I'm cheering you on. Go get it.

Carrie Williams

About the Author

Carrie Williams is a leadership coach, public speaker, facilitator, and author who specializes in working with creative and entertainment companies and legal entrepreneurs across the globe. Carrie is proud to have helped thousands of clients and associates set and achieve life changing goals with her G.R.E.A.T. Goals program.

She is the founder of Los Angeles based RainShadow Coaching, which is dedicated to helping professionals and companies forge their own living masterpiece, by focusing on the three tiers of fulfillment: professional success, personal growth, and overall well-being.

Carrie is a certified PCC with the ICF (International Coach Federation), and holds a graduate certification in evidence-based coaching from Fielding Graduate University.

Williams currently lives in Los Angeles with her husband and their cat, Senator Biscuit Whiskily Tiskers.

Resources and Inspiration

Bridges, W. (2004). *Transitions: Making Sense of Life's Changes.* Cambridge: Perseus Books.

Bridges, W., & Bridges, S. (2009). *Managing Transitions: Making the Most of Change.* Cambridge: Perseus.

Baumeister, R. F., & Tierney, J. (2012). *Willpower: Rediscovering the Greatest Human Strength.* New York: Penguin.

Dweck, C. S. (2006). *Mindset: The New Psychology of Success: How We Can Learn to Fulfill Our Potential.* New York: Ballantine.

Fredrickson, B. L. (2009). *Positivity: Groundbreaking Research Reveals How to Embrace the Hidden Strength of Positive Emotions, Overcome Negativity, and Thrive.* New York: Crown.

Fredrickson, B. L. (2014). *Love 2.0: Creating Happiness and Health in Moments of Connection.* New York: Penguin.

Rath, T., & Harter, J. (2010). *Wellbeing: The Five Essential Elements.* New York: Gallup.

Kegan, R., & Laskow Lahey, L. (2009). *Immunity to Change: How to Overcome It and Unlock the Potential in Yourself and Your Organization.* Boston: Harvard Business Press.

Seligman, M. E. P. (2011). *Flourish: A Visionary New Understanding of Happiness and Well-being.* New York: Atria.

Seligman, M. E. P. (2002). *Authentic Happiness: Using the New Positive Psychology to Realize Your Potential for Lasting Fulfillment.* New York: Free Press.

Sinek, S. (2011). *Start with Why: How Great Leaders Inspire Everyone to Take Action.* New York: Penguin.

51845127R00071

Made in the USA
San Bernardino, CA
03 August 2017